ABOUT THE

Dr Michael Hewitt-Gleeson is a Melbourne-based author, motivational speaker and cognitive scientist, whose research has been in designing human thinking strategies and what he calls 'software for the brain'. In 1979 he co-founded the School of Thinking in New York City with Dr Edward de Bono and in 1980, Dr de Bono was Michael's tutor for the world's first PhD in Lateral Thinking. Since then, Michael's training lessons have reached over 70 million people worldwide. He is acknowledged for having provided the theoretical base for the current trend of 'customer-driven' strategies which informed sales and marketing in the 1980s and '90s and led to the evolution of darwinian marketing, e-commerce, permission marketing and viral marketing.

By the same author

Software for Your Brain

The X10 Memeplex

NewSell

Clever

Learn-To-Think
(with Edward de Bono)

WOMBAT SELLING

How to sell by Word of Mouth

MICHAEL HEWITT-GLEESON

Hardie Grant Books

Every effort has been made to incorporate correct information and statistics. The author and publisher regret any errors and omissions and invite readers to contribute up-to-date or additional relevant information to Hardie Grant Books.

Published in Australia in 2006
by Hardie Grant Books
85 High Street
Prahran, Victoria 3181, Australia
www.hardiegrant.com.au

First published in 1990 under the title *NewSell* by WrightBooks

National Library of Australia Cataloguing-in-Publication Data:
Hewitt-Gleeson, Michael, 1947– .
WOMBAT selling.
Rev. ed.
Bibliography.
ISBN 1 74066 428 0 (pbk.).
1. Selling. I. Title.
658.85

Cover and internal design by Pigs Might Fly Productions
Typesetting by Kirby Jones
Printed and bound in Australia by Griffin Press
10 9 8 7 6 5 4 3 2 1

For Augustine,
Gallup and
Berners-Lee

Contents

Introduction

In life, there are two kinds of theories and two ways to accept them. One kind of theory is supported by evidence and can be accepted through observation. The other kind is not supported by evidence and must be accepted on faith. The traditional theory of selling (which I have called 'oldsell') is based on a long-held fundamental belief about selling/marketing that is unsupported by evidence. It can be summed up in one simple sentence: *The salesperson closes the sale.*

There is no evidence to support this theory so it is accepted on faith and taught to young salespeople in Australia, the US and many other countries around the world.

For 30 years I have been spreading what I call the 'newsell' option. Newsell is an alternative theory of selling/marketing that can be measured so it can be accepted by observation. Newsell works on the following premise: *The customer closes the sale.*

In newsell there are three main 'attitudes':

- the science of selling/marketing is 'word-of-mouth' not 'closing-the-sale'
- the customer rules so try never to forget it
- your customers' word-of-mouth can help you multiply the '10 per cent growth' pattern by a factor of ten, so it becomes the 'X10 growth' pattern.

I am an author and a motivational speaker. I am also a scientist. The two main features associated with this kind of job are teaching and travel. For the past 50 years, the three subjects that I've been most interested in are thinking, selling and leadership. I was introduced to them when I was eight. I started teaching them in Melbourne when I was 16. Since then, these three fascinating human faculties are what I've been most often invited to speak about around the world, and now I'm 59.

As you would expect, my niche market has consisted of aspirational thinkers – those middle-class people who desire a better life and who want better things, especially those who are able to do something about it. I've taught parents, educators, scientists, employees, entrepreneurs, CEOs, preachers, politicians, artists and elite sportspeople. The reason aspirational thinkers require motivation is because they know they can do better, they want to do better and so they seek out teachers who might be able to show them a better way.

This quest began one summer when I was 16 and saw an ad in the paper for a part-time selling job: 'we'll train you, no experience necessary'. The ad was for an American company who sold insurance policies to small businesses door-to-door. I lasted about four weeks. Most recruits lasted about two. This was my first exposure to the high-pressure American model of selling, a model which is based on exhorting the salesperson to close the sale.

This model didn't work then in Australia and it doesn't work now, but I was too young to know that. Little did I realise that one day I would formally challenge that idea and prove it to be false. However, I was bright, keen to learn and willing to work at it and so were most of the other recruits. The sales trainers and managers were dogmatic and heavy-handed; they kept urging us to close, close, close. However, no matter how often we repeated the company's script to our laconic 'prospects', they just said NO.

Naturally I thought it was me, just like Willy Loman in *Death of A Salesman*. But I knew I was doing everything the American bosses taught me ... meticulously. Still, the customers kept saying NO. Eventually, I became discouraged and started to avoid making calls. I'd go to a movie instead. Ultimately, I quit. At the time, I thought it was a waste of a summer. My friends all said so. And my dad teased me endlessly: 'Do you know where I can get some insurance, Mike?'

As it turned out, it wasn't a waste of time. My sales trainer gave me a classic American motivational book called *Think and Grow Rich* by Napoleon Hill. In this book, the author had studied the thoughts, behaviour and philosophies of a significant selection of successful American business leaders and had interviewed a number of millionaires (a million dollars was a lot in those days). You can still find the book in the self-help section of most bookstores. The main idea that came out of it was this: What the mind can conceive and believe it can achieve. In 1963, this was a very exotic idea for a boy like me – the explicit connection between thinking and accomplishment. I remember wondering if this could be literally true. Although uncertain, I decided to invest in the concept; the implications for my whole life and future would surely be enormous if it worked.

Abbreviating the message into 'CBA' (Conceive Believe Achieve) I set about programming it into my mind through daily repetition. Learning Latin vocabulary at boarding school had already shown me the practical effectiveness that repetition has on the human mind. CBA certainly did work for me, often enough, to be one of the most useful tools I have ever distilled. Many times since then I have used the CBA thinking skill in a very deliberate way to make my life more interesting – sometimes for profit, often for fun and nearly always as a premeditated experiment to demonstrate its effectiveness. I have found CBA to be a lot like a useful investment strategy – it doesn't work every time but it works often enough to make it worthwhile.

The door-to-door selling experience also made me curious about the theory of 'selling' and the excesses of the American business culture. I began to read up on it. Most of the books were the same. They were full of exhortation and closing techniques. There were big promises of success if you believed, and threats of failure if you didn't. Success or failure. Right or wrong. Black or white. Heaven or Hell. Hmmm. This was vaguely familiar. Where had I heard all this before?

It was another decade before I really understood the religious fervour behind the American sales training model. It arose out of Middle America in the '40s and '50s and was based on the American version of the bible. Indeed, many of the US sales gurus were also preachers, men like Norman Vincent Peale, Robert Schuller and Zig Ziglar. I nicknamed this approach oldsell. By this time I was living in the US and was teaching a heretical sales training strategy of my own which I called newsell. They were amazed. These 'Australian heresies' were getting much better sales results. And this was well before Crocodile Dundee came along.

WOMBAT Selling (WOMBAT stands for **W**ord **O**f **M**outh **B**uy **A**nd **T**ell) explains the difference between oldsell and newsell in today's business world. Earlier editions of this book, published under the title *NewSell*, came out in 1990 and 1994. This new edition develops the WOMBAT sales and marketing strategy which is all about selling by word of mouth. Everyone is a WOMBAT, all the time. This is the biggest insight from this book and by Part Three you should be able to get it and the more you get this insight, the more you'll get from this book. Here it is again: Everyone is a WOMBAT. All the time!

WOMBAT Selling has only a tenth of the information that I'd like to put into it but I'm told that customers don't want thick tomes anymore so there's no sense in publishing them. However, I have included additional information in my Newsell Coaching Program at *www.newsellcoaching.com* for those who are interested. For this edition I have synthesized the best of all the earlier editions and introduced some new developments since the Internet and e-commerce have so suddenly and dramatically changed the business environment. This book is designed for anyone interested in selling and leadership, especially those who are interacting with customers.

If you really want to upgrade your selling and marketing skills then you not only have to change the way you think about how you *sell*, but you also have to change the way you think about how you *think*. This is why there is such a strong link between thinking, selling and leadership.

The purpose of this book is to change the way you think about selling (and leadership, which is just another kind of selling). Robert Louis Stevenson once said, 'Everyone is a salesman'. This is truer today than ever before. Everyone is a customer, that's for sure. The mood of the market has evolved from the salesperson-centered approach of the 1950s as promoted in the US, to the customer-centered approach of the 1980s as promoted in Australia, and now the *meme*-centered approach of the 2000s as promoted in cyberspace by search engines like Google and Yahoo. It continues to evolve.

Growth is critical to all business. Things can't stay the same because the market is always changing. You're either growing or you're shrinking. If you are like most people, business growth in your brain is governed by the current growth pattern of '10 per cent per annum' – an idea which came out of the Industrial Revolution. But, of course, things have changed dramatically since then ...

- What if this is the beginning of the science/technology boom not the end?
- What if the largest generation in history – the boomers – are now in their peak spending years?
- What if anyone in the world could do business with you with the press of a button?
- What if the world wide market came to your personal desktop?
- What if your business is only a tenth of what it will be in the next few years?
- What if your next computer is ten times more powerful than your last one?
- What if your productivity is on the verge of a quantum leap?
- What if your customers became your best, most credible salespeople?
- What if we are just at the beginning of the beginning of the new renaissance?

There are many different and interesting ways that readers have used the new kind of sales training presented in this book to accelerate the growth of their business. This new kind of sales training is called newsell.

Newsell goes beyond traditional sales training. It is *not* of the oldsell-type, evangelical, high pressure, motivational, quasi-religious kind. Research shows again and again that most customers reject these old-fashioned 'closing-the-sale' ploys and car-salesman tricks that originated in Middle America in the '50s. This new kind of sales training was developed in the relatively small but sophisticated Australian market and then exported to the US in the '80s and '90s.

Newsell is young, fast and scientific. It is also professional, relaxed and ethical, but the results are commercial, immediate and measurable. Newsell has produced ten times the results of the oldsell methods!

Michael Hewitt-Gleeson
Wye River
Autumn 2006

1

The Close
AND
the Oldsell
Strategy

NOTE: On Acronyms and Repetition

To help transfer the ideas from this book into your brain – so you can put them into use – you will notice I use acronyms to encapsulate ideas and repetition to create cognitive patterns. Some people dislike acronyms because they can seem jargonistic. Others may be averse to repetition because it can seem tedious. This is understandable, especially in a novel. But in this book we are concerned with skill development, that's why the military, NASA, the Juillard School, the Russian Ballet, top surgeons, Circus Oz, the Australian Institute of Sports – in fact, all the sports and performing arts – readily use these two powerful training tools. If you only wish to know about newsell these two training tools are not necessary. If you wish to be able to do newsell as a skill, they are indispensable.

Below is a list of the principal acronyms used in this book:

CVSTOBVS (CVS to BVS) – the thinking switch
    CVS = Current View of the Situation
    BVS = Better View of the Situation

UNCHECKTOCHECK (UNCHECK to CHECK) – the
    selling switch
    UNCHECK = when not in contact with a
        customer
    CHECK = when in contact with a customer

TCB – alternative to 'the close'
    TCB = Taking Care of Business

COI – an individual who influences ten other
    people
    COI = Centre of Influence

WOMBAT – a satisfied customer who replicates
    another satisfied customer
    WOMBAT = Word Of Mouth Buy And Tell

TT Management System
    T = TODAY = total number of times you did
        move from Uncheck to Check in past
        24 hours
    T = TOMORROW = total number of times you
        will move from Uncheck to Check in next
        24 hours

IMPORTANT MEMO TO CEOS FROM
michael@newsellcoaching.com

Since I first wrote *NewSell* in 1984, two unique and very big things have happened. Unique because nothing like them have ever happened before in history; very big because they have created brand new multi-billion dollar global industries with vast potential. Both have profoundly impacted global business and will continue to do. These two things are:

● the world wide web with its creation of e-commerce, and
● the mapping of the human genome and the creation of biotechnology.

I want to begin with a word of warning to CEOs about the Internet and the whole new ballgame of e-commerce.

While CEOs admit that the Internet has an impact on the reputation of their company, very few are doing anything about it. That's the conclusion of one of the largest surveys of CEOs' attitudes to corporate reputation conducted by Chief Executive magazine. Of the 600 CEOs and senior managers interviewed, less than half had a deliberate Internet strategy for managing their corporate image.

More than 60 per cent of CEOs were very concerned about negative word-of-mouth but only 11 per cent actually monitor the Net to understand what is being said about their companies and their brands. Forty per cent said their biggest concern was about unhappy customers venting their dissatisfaction online. Twenty-five per cent were concerned about both ex-employees and current employees using the Internet to criticise their companies. It's a virtual jungle out there and many companies, even big ones, are not surviving. Of the Fortune 500 class of 1974, only 22 were still around in 2004.

In the context of how to survive and grow in the world-wide darwinian marketplace, I want to begin this book with these fundamental 'wake-up and smell the coffee' points. Some of these thoughts were inspired after reading *The Cluetrain Manifesto*:

- Darwinian marketing is a battle of ideas not a battle of products.
- Owning an idea in the customer's mind over a longer period of time is the #1 goal of darwinian marketing.
- It's better to be first in the mind than first in the media.
- It's better for your idea to be a word-of-mouth than an advertisement.
- If your customers are not replicating themselves by word-of-mouth you have little chance of surviving on the Internet.
- A market is an idea-pool. A market is an idea exchange among human beings, receiving and exchanging their ideas by word-of-mouth.

- The Internet is a wired idea-pool. Your company intranet is a wired idea-pool.
- Wired idea-pools are much faster and therefore much smarter than traditional markets.
- The current balance of ideas in the online idea-pool is often the opposite of what appears in the traditional mass media.
- No union can organise knowledge-workers the way the idea-pool of a company's intranet allows the workers to organise themselves.
- There are two concurrent idea-pools: one inside the company via the intranet and one with the market via the Internet. These two idea-pools eventually spill into each other. Your knowledge-workers talk to your customers in their own way every day.
- Via the Internet and the intranet, customers and employees are using word-of-mouth to exchange ideas in an independent and powerful new way.
- Word-of-mouth means swapping jokes by email, opinions by voicemail, gossip by SMS and argument by all kinds of human interaction sometimes above the radar more often below it.
- Interactive word-of-mouth is compelling to other humans in a way which is not possible from vendors in the mass media, yet many CEOs still squander their marketing budgets on traditional mass media in the traditional way.
- The idea-pool has all the ideas of all the companies and whether the news is good or bad they can infect anyone by word-of-mouth.

- Companies who contribute poorly to the idea-pool find the markets are often ridiculing their ideas.
- Vendors who offer better ideas will survive better in the darwinian marketplace.
- The wired idea-pool, even at its worst, is more compelling than most business meetings or trade shows and certainly more intimate than corporate advertising campaigns.
- To traditional oldsell corporations, the wired idea-pool may appear chaotic but it is organising much faster than they are and evolving with much better tools and many more ideas.
- The wired idea-pool is linking people to each other – *peer2peer* – 24/7. It's not waiting for those who are left behind.
- In darwinian marketing, your reputation as an attractive and innovative idea-fountain is everything. It's your survival advantage in the idea-pool. Protect it at all costs.
- In darwinian marketing, attractive bait ideas that bring people to you are useful and ideas that gain attention are very powerful ideas.
- Ideas that show generosity are attractive to people and will keep them near you.
- Ideas that appeal to the patience or forbearance of humans do not survive up against ideas that appeal to people's self-interest and to their fantasies.

And this is just the beginning ...

The Challenge

How can dividing your sales team in two halves double your profits?

The existing Theory of Selling is:
- **You Close the Sale**

The Newsell Theory of Selling is:
- **You Cannot Close the sale**

There is a world of difference between the two theories.
Which one is more productive?
Flashback: Melbourne, Australia, 3 August 1998
Yesterday, I visited 'The Builder of Sales Champions'
Mr Tom Hopkins' webpage where he claims to show you

how to 'close the sale' for $US24.95 in his book *How To Master The Art of Selling*. Today, because he's currently in Melbourne on a lecture tour, I have publicly challenged Mr Hopkins – with a reward of $100,000 – if he can show me how to close the sale.

Tom didn't take up the challenge, which still stands. It was reported in the *Herald Sun* newspaper.

BID TO TOP EXPERT'S PITCH
A $100,000 challenge has been issued to visiting American pitchmaster Tom Hopkins, who will speak to a sellout audience of more than 2000 at the Dallas Brooks Centre on Monday. Melbourne business motivator Dr Michael Hewitt-Gleeson says he will give the money 'to the charity of Mr. Hopkin's choice if he can prove that the salesperson closes the sale'. But how does Hopkins, who has shared the stage with such motivators as General 'Stormin" Norman Schwarzkopf, prove that the salesman closes the sale? 'Well, if he can, it will be worth the $100,000,' said Hewitt-Gleeson. 'It would win the Nobel Prize.'

In this book you'll see why I made that challenge. Why it's so misleading to give young salespeople the impression that their job is to 'close the sale'. Why this theory, which I have called oldsell, has produced such poor sales results and made a laughing stock of the selling profession. Why customers hate this approach and what you can do to escape from this old-fashioned idea.

The new millennium calls for a new approach to selling. Customers are not dumb. The daily supermarket shopper has more than 25 choices just for buying milk! Don't expect customers who can shop globally online for a new computer to take seriously the childish antics of the door-to-door bible salesman.

To begin, here are a few of the tips we'll be using that will help you move away from oldsell towards newsell:

1 Your salespeople don't close the sale

In reality, this medieval dogma of 'closing the sale' is a nonsense that is taught to salespeople as novices and accepted by them as a sacred belief – and unfortunately, it seems very few challenge that belief ever again. Like an information virus that gets into their brains, 'closing the sale' influences young salespeople's behaviour and dominates their sales activities. The costly failure of this 'close-the-sale' strategy is well documented and nothing has so damaged the image of the sales profession than this selling disease. It's difficult to see how young salespeople could be misled more than to be given the impression that their job is to 'close the sale'.

FACT: *You* cannot close the sale. The decision to buy is an electro-chemical event that takes place in the brain of the customer. The salesperson cannot control that event. What the salesperson *can* do however, is to create an opportunity for that event to happen – making a sales call.

FACT: The salesperson opens the sale by making the call, the customer closes the sale by deciding to buy – YES – or not to buy – NO.

2   Focus your efforts on how to get the customer's attention

Before a customer can say YES or NO we first have to get his or her attention. There's always been the problem of attention in selling but now it's getting worse. In any marketplace, every trader competes with every other trader for the attention of the customer. It is obvious that before a trader can make an offer they first have to get the attention of the potential buyer. Visit a flea market, a fish market, a supermarket or a stock market and see the enormous amount of selling effort which is directed to getting and holding the attention of the customer. This is mostly done through *brain branding*.

A brand is a corporate cognitive pattern. The pattern links a brain directly to a corporation. Brain branding, using repetition, is the programming of a corporate cognitive pattern – a brand – in the brain of a customer. This is done through the power of repetition. When a minimum of 10 repetitions of a brand takes place in a customer's brain, the pattern becomes *cognised* and later can be recognised and used as part of the customer's experience. Brain branding makes it easier to attract the future attention of the consumer. As you'll see, the key is repetition.

Looking back from the end of any transaction – when the customer buys – there is always a track winding back to attention. Attracting and holding attention has always been a problem in selling and as the information big bang gathers momentum it becomes harder and harder to secure 'share of attention'. Why? Because there are:

● more TV channels than ever before
● more magazines than ever before
● more ads than ever before
● more offers than ever before
● less 'attention share' than ever before.

Your selling has to become cleverer and cleverer at getting and holding attention. In a true darwinian sense, only the fittest offers can survive and the edge of an offer is attention.

In the new millennium we are surfing through cyberia. We don't wade through information anymore.

There's too much. Today, whether it's snail mail or email, the issue in selling is how to get the surfer's attention and hold on to it long enough to send a message. In newsell we do this by using a binary switch – a mental thought process – for which I've borrowed terms from the game of chess. I call it going from the position of UNCHECK to the position of CHECK.

3 Escape from the Darkness of Uncheck

We use three terms in newsell theory. In newsell the primary focus is on the Check move. Check signifies a customer contact. The Check position simply means the position when you are actually in contact with a customer or prospective customer. Check is the quintessence of the newsell strategy, it's the moment of customer contact. Check is when you contact a customer with your offer and so the customer can now say either YES or NO. And, they do.

The other two terms are Checkmate and Uncheck. Checkmate is when the customer says YES. This is the same as 'the close' in oldsell or traditional selling. Uncheck is when there is no contact with a customer or prospect so the customer cannot say either YES or NO.

Research shows that Uncheck is the default or stable position. Most of the time, most of the salespeople are in a state of Uncheck with most of the customers. At any particular moment most salespeople are not in contact with most prospects. They are in Uncheck. As I sit here writing this book I am in Uncheck and as you sit reading it you are in Uncheck, too.

To summarise:

- Checkmate = when the customer says YES
- Check = when the customer says YES or NO
- Uncheck = when the customer CANNOT say either YES or NO.

FACT: The customer controls checkmate. Only the customer can say YES. Traditional oldsell doesn't understand this fact of science and thinks this is where the action is for salespeople. Big mistake!

FACT: The salesperson controls Check. Check makes it possible for the customer to say YES or NO. In newsell, Check is where the action is. Uncheck is whenever, at any time, you are not in contact with a customer.

FACT: No-one controls Uncheck because there is just NO CONTACT between the salesperson and the customer. Therefore, it's impossible for the customer to say YES or NO. Like the 99 per cent of dark matter in the universe, this is the darkness of the business world. This is where all the failures take place in selling. Uncheck is your enemy, not the customer. Love your customer and escape from Uncheck.

Newsell is a digital switch. Like other digital switches it has two positions – Uncheck to Check. When you flip it you slide from one universe (Uncheck) where you can *never* get a YES or a NO to another universe (Check) where you can *always* get a YES or a NO. And guess what? Only you control the switch. The newsell switch, pronounced as three words 'Uncheck to Check', has its own logo – UNCHECKTOCHECK.

4   Quarterly Projections and Daily Measurement of Check moves

Check is the fundamental business move, the basic unit of business measurement. Yet, in 25 years of consulting, I've never found a company that knows exactly how many Check moves it makes each business quarter, how often they flip the switch from Uncheck to Check.

FACT: Sales are a direct consequence of customer contacts. If we use quarterly sales projections why don't we use quarterly projections for customer contacts, for Check moves? To help escape from the darkness of Uncheck and take control of your business, make quarterly projections of your Check moves and keep daily measurements of how often you flip the switch. It's possible to do (we'll show you how in this book) and always raises the sales activity – UNCHECKTOCHECK.

5 Use Tenpower – Add a Zero!

In the School of Thinking at schoolofthinking.org we teach our students how to use 'Tenpower' to gain an advantage over their competitors. Tenpower is the habit of using Powers of Ten. One way to use tenpower is to habitually multiply by ten (X10) or add a zero – to whatever it is you are doing.

Tenpower helps you escape from Uncheck. You can tenpower any Check move you are planning to make. You can go for the quantum leap. If you want to win, escape from Uncheck and do so ten times more often than your competitor. UNCHECKTOCHECK X10 = Newsell.

This book shows you, step by step, how to do all this. And, to help you program your brain enough to put these strategies into action, I've included lots of repetition. Enjoy!

6 Divide Your Sales Team and Double Your Profits

Because the marketplace is continually evolving, your business strategies must never stagnate. You must constantly be experimenting and testing new ways, different methods, even old ideas in new settings and watching carefully what happens. Add your wins to your expanding repertoire and harvest valuable insights from your inevitable flops and mistakes. Mistakes, in this context, are good. The only trap is to stand still, marking time.

Every day is a unique chance to use your sales team to test new ideas. You can try fresh newsell experiments anytime by using this simple four-step process:

1 Divide your sales team randomly in two equal halves (for example, by birthdays: odd days and even days will divide them randomly).

2 Leave one half of the team on their current diet of sales training as a control. Make no changes at all. Put the other half on a diet of newsell.

3 Choose the metrics in advance you want to test. Choose the top three key performance indicators you will use to judge the outcome.

4 Compare the results after 10 days and 100 days.

2

Melbourne, Australia

How can an Australian teach Americans anything about selling?

'I am aware when even the brightest mind in our world has been trained up from childhood in a superstition of any kind, it will never be possible for that mind, in its maturity, to examine sincerely, dispassionately, and conscientiously any evidence or any circumstance which shall seem to cast a doubt upon the validity of that superstition.'
– Mark Twain, American thinker and humorist

One question that has arisen from time to time during my career has been this: 'How can an Australian go to the US and teach Americans how to sell?' Interestingly, this is asked more often in Australia than anywhere else. When I first went to the US – the Land of the Salesman – I went to learn, not to teach. But I was surprised by what I found – even though Australia might be a small country, it has a lot to offer our big cousins in the US and Europe and our good neighbours in China and South East Asia.

The City of Melbourne is home of the Melbourne Cup where the mini-skirt was invented. It's the home of Victoria Bitter and the HQ of the Aussie Rules football code. It is sometimes described as the Intellectual Capital of Australia. The first line of the Australian national song, 'Australians all let us rejoice for we are young and free' was beamed around the world, many times, during the Sydney Olympics in 2000. Australia is even called the 'Lucky Country' because it is a young nation and its citizens enjoy a freedom that is unprecedented. This is something we should not take for granted.

Freedom of Choice

In Melbourne, as in other parts of Australia, there are over 270 distinct religious groups. This is evidence of the creativity, tolerance and goodwill of our nation. In part, it is made possible by Section 116 of the Australian Constitution which states that all religions are equal under the Law of Australia. In Australia no single religion can ever be the 'one true religion'. We share the long evolution of the Aboriginal Dreaming, the wisdom gained from the suffering of Judaism, the warmth of the brotherhood of Islam, the charity of the Christians with their love of God and fellow humans beings, the peace and compassion of Buddhism, the pluralism of the Hindus, the Taoist respect of nature, the emphasis on relationships and manners of Confucianism, the social justice of Marxism, the humanist freedom of the liberals, the holistic approach of the Africans, the Sikhs with their humour and sincerity and, a growing number of Australians – more than 25 per cent – who are free to state that they practise no religion at all.

These religious systems are a priceless part of our vast treasure of intellectual capital. All these diverse religious values have thrived and are compatible in an environment of mutual respect and freedom. As a young country, we have learned from the bitter experience of others. We have seen that it is only when one religion seeks to impose its authority and righteousness over another that we can expect the brutality and the terror of religious wars and crusades, the horror of fatwahs and inquisitions, and the fury of the persecutions that follow.

So what then is the quintessential benefit of Section 116? It is, simply, freedom of choice. That means freedom for you to choose, not for someone else to choose for you.

But Australians are not blind. As with many nations, we have seen the practice fall short of the ideal. Australia can reflect on its own sorry history of discrimination and persecutions – the floggings of Irish convicts, the 'pig tailing' of the Chinese, the theft of Aboriginal children, the schism of the Labour movement, the treatment of Vietnam veterans, and the White Australia Policy. Still, the ideal of Freedom of Religion is quintessentially Australian and it is one that I personally have always supported.

This freedom also means we are free to explore, discuss and even challenge those ancient ideas that were exported to Australia from Europe, Asia and other cultures. To do this we use the tools of science. Why? What is it that makes science so unique? What is it that separates the scientific approach to matters from other non-scientific approaches?

The answer is: testing and measuring.

The Balance of Evidence

It's only by putting a theory up against testing and measuring that we can move it from science fiction towards science fact. I say *towards* because we can never actually prove anything in science in an absolute sense.

What we can say is that after testing and measurement of the evidence, the balance of evidence as it now stands would indicate that such-and-such a theory seems valid. It's a 'more likely truth'. This always gets updated at a later stage by other scientists as testing and measuring procedures improve and as new theories, new 'more likely truths', are put forward.

The absence of testing and measuring is: faith. When we are in a non-scientific mode we can use faith as a way of coming to a point-of-view. There are many things in human culture that don't lend themselves very well to testing and measuring and some people still derive value from believing in them.

In the metaphysical marketplace there exists a myriad of myths and legends, folklore, superstitions and fortune telling, plus a rich collection of supernatural heroes and beliefs. These have provided a great deal of interest to millions of people even though (maybe because) many of these areas elude any form of objective testing or measurement.

For example, no-one has ever been able to test or measure the existence of 'guardian angels'. So this is an unscientific belief that can be simply accepted on faith if one chooses to do so. Some people take comfort in the idea of having a guardian angel and it may be a benefit to them. Others find the concept unwelcome. The thought of being stalked 24/7 by a spiritual Peeping Tom may seem an infringement on one's personal liberty!

It was recently estimated by a religious leader that around 30 per cent of the world's population derive value and comfort from religious beliefs of one kind or another. Most of these believers were born into major world religions like Judaism, Christianity, Islam, Hinduism or Buddhism. In addition, there is a vast array of smaller religions, cults and belief systems which testify to the richness and diversity of human imagination.

These belief systems require believers to take a leap of faith and to believe in things that we may not be able to test or measure. These beliefs fall outside the scientific method. This doesn't necessarily mean their claims are not true or didn't happen, it simply means that the balance of evidence is so slim that we have no way of knowing whether they are true and so, if we accept them, we do so by taking a leap of faith. Many people are quite able to take such a leap of faith while others may have had a set of beliefs culturally programmed into their brain when they were young.

To be considered scientifically valid, a proposition must be able to be tested or measured independently. It is not enough to simply measure the number of people who believe it. Just because a million people believe the earth is flat is not enough to make it flat. If a million becomes ten million the earth will still not lose its third dimension.

Memes, Replicators and Ideaviruses

Memes are idea viruses – ideas that self-replicate. Memes are the only other replicator, besides genes, yet discovered by science. The word meme is pronounced like 'theme'. The Oxford English Dictionary defines a gene as 'a unit of heredity ... that determines a particular characteristic of an individual' and a meme as 'a self-replicating element of culture, passed on by imitation'. To that definition should also be added the meaning of the verb:

> **meme** v to infect with a meme (The CEO memed his employees with a personal email.)

Memes are stored in our brains and passed on by imitation. For example, Richard Dawkins points to 'tunes, ideas, catch-phrases, clothes fashions, ways of making pots or of building arches'. He also considers religions to be among the most powerful of these mind viruses.

We may simply believe things because we have been memed. We may think we know things because we were told to believe them or just because we never really thought the matter through ourselves. A belief may really only be an area that has been protected from thinking for many years.

The Moses Meme

Long before I was old enough to really think the matter through, I had been memed, as a small child, with the theory of Moses. It went something like this: Moses was a leader in ancient times and, like all leaders, he needed his people to adhere to his laws. He said that his ten laws or commandments should be obeyed. The reason that they should be obeyed, he claimed, was because they were given to him, privately, on a mountain, by his god, Yahweh. By making this claim, Moses positioned his ten laws with the highest possible authority. They were not his laws, said Moses, but God's.

This is a very old story that many people, like me, just accepted but have never really updated or thought through properly. I had never really thought much about the Moses story until I was given an antique gift. It was a heavy Victorian cast-iron desk ornament about half a metre long which was grotesquely dominated by a 50-centimetre high copy of Michelangelo's Moses supported by two large topped blown-glass inkwells and a generous ladle for pens. It was absurdly out of place on my desk in my small Park Avenue South apartment but I liked it. Moses lorded over my desk in New York City for ten years until eventually I returned to Australia. Sadly, it was one of the many things that I left behind. But for most of the '80s I sat and stared at Moses nearly every day. Eventually, I began to think more and more about the theory of Moses.

What is the theory of Moses? This is just one of the five most obvious questions. We cannot explore that question without the other four: Who was Moses? What did Moses do? How did he do it? And, when and where did he do it?

If you do stop to think about this story in the light of evidence available today you might ask yourself for a more plausible version. Since there were no witnesses or evidence of any kind we don't know whether Moses' version actually happened. Yet there is much evidence to show that it is very unlikely.

Three of the world's major religions – the 'one God meme' of Judaism, Islam and Christianity – are evolved variations of 'monotheism'. However, the first recorded evidence of this meme from which all the above versions have evolved arises only about a hundred years before Moses. It was King Tut's father, the pharaoh Akhenaton, who was the inventor of monotheism. Although Moses gets all the credit, the evidence shows that this heretic king invented the first monotheistic meme about 3000 years ago.

Many scholars have written about this, not the least of whom Sigmund Freud, the founder of psychoanalysis, who wrote in *Moses and Monotheism* that the real Moses was born an Egyptian prince not a Jewish slave and had become a monotheist, after Akhenaton. In his opening paragraph Freud writes:

'To deny a people the man whom it praises as the greatest of its sons is not a deed to be undertaken lightheartedly – especially by one belonging to that people. No consideration, however, will move me to set aside truth in favour of national interests. Moreover, the elucidation of the mere facts of the problem may be expected to deepen our insight into the situation with which they are concerned.'

Throughout the millennia of human cultural evolution there is much evidence proving the invention by thinkers of thousands of such 'black-box memes'. These memes evolved to fill the needs of the brain to make some sense of the inexplicable physics of the world. Take for instance the 'god memes' that modern man has invented over the last 100,000 years, such as the 'Zeus meme' to explain the phenomenon of lightning or the 'god of the Nile' meme to explain why the Nile flooded from time to time. On New Year's Day 2005, amidst the tragedy and destruction of the Indian Ocean tsunami, some people claimed it was an act of God. A poll, conducted by *The Age* newspaper in Melbourne, returned the following results:

Faith and disasters

Question: Has the tsunami shaken your faith in God?

No, it is all part of God's plan	12 per cent
No, evil things happen despite the power of God	18 per cent
No, my faith is strengthened by the world's response	14 per cent
Yes, a caring God would never let this happen	3 per cent
Yes, I have now lost all faith in God	2 per cent
I don't believe in God. This was a natural phenomenon	52 per cent
Total Votes:	2072

There are many examples of how the clever human brain has evolved its role as an effective explanation-creating mechanism. This is not the same thing as explaining the actual phenomena. Just because a meme has infected millions of brains is not enough reason, by itself, to make the meme a truth. There needs to be the balance of evidence that enables us to differentiate the false memes from the truer memes. In fact, if you think about it, there are many possible explanations that could explain the Moses meme and how he came up with his commandments. Some that have been suggested by other thinkers are:

- Moses sought authority over his people and was clever enough to make up the story to give his laws more authority
- Moses just dreamt it
- Moses might have been euphoric or hallucinating from inhaling smoke from a nearby burning bush
- Moses may have been overtired
- Exhaustion or malnutrition may have impaired Moses' judgment
- Old Moses may have been suffering from Alzheimer's or one of a range of infirmities or mental illnesses
- The whole story was invented not by Moses at all but by people who came after Moses.

In other words, we simply just don't know for certain. However, millions of people who adhere to the Judeo-Christian tradition have chosen to take a leap of faith and to believe the traditional Moses claim. A Christian or Jewish scientist could not accept this story as a scientist, but could accept it, on a leap of faith, as part of a religious belief system.

Science + Religion

The argument between science and religion is a false one. It is simply a matter of distinguishing between those things we believe because we have tested them and are part of science, and those things we believe because we cannot test them so we take a leap of faith. In a free country, there is no reason why we cannot hold viewpoints in both areas as long as we are able to distinguish between the two. Most American books on selling come from a religious tradition. To help restore the balance a little, this book on selling comes out of science.

The Unclaimed Reward

How can a salesperson win $100,000 *and* a Nobel Prize?

I first used the $100,000 challenge back in the late '80s. I was invited by National Mutual, the then number two Australian life insurance company, to be the keynote speaker at a sales conference in Phuket, Thailand. This event was a reward for the company's top-performing insurance agents. The group consisted of 120 men and women all earning between $200,000 and $2 million in commissions per annum. Needless to say, the highlights of the conference were the beach and the sun, the surf and the sails, the pool and the cocktail bar. But, to make it tax-deductible, they had to have a 'motivational speaker'.

Formally introduced as 'Dr Michael Hewitt-Gleeson', I staged a ponderous walk to the lectern with a large pile of notes, looking every bit the academic. I peered out over my glasses, paused for effect and then said, 'Let me start by saying that there's no such thing as closing the sale!'

You can imagine the reaction. The body language was not subtle. They were saying, 'Can you believe this?' and 'Where do they get these nerds from?' They were outraged at the suggestion. Here they were, all national champions. They wouldn't even be here if they weren't champion closers and now this jerk was claiming you couldn't close the sale.

I continued. 'Look, I'm not going to attempt to argue with you about this claim because we could do so all day, never get anywhere, waste our time and miss out on the beach. So, I'll tell you what I'll do. I'll give $100,000 cash,' at this point I took out a fat wad of notes, 'to the first person who can prove that you, the salesperson, closes the sale. Here I am. Here's the cash. Come and close me now!'

Then an interesting thing happened. Nothing. Not a single champion salesperson approached the lectern.

I was talking later to one of the leading agents who said, 'I couldn't believe it. There I was getting ready to run up and claim the cash. I tried to think what I could say or do to make you say YES. I couldn't think.' He then added, 'And, to my horror, not one person in a room of 120 national champions was able to do it either.'

This was the first time I had ever tried this stunt and I've done it many times since. It worked well and I had their undivided attention for the next two hours while I showed them the difference between the traditional American selling theory, oldsell (which they believed in), and newsell. The cash motive in the stunt also helped them to keep their minds open and be less defensive about their current point-of-view.

For my part, it gave me an invaluable insight. When they first started out, these people had all been taught the fundamental belief in selling that their job was to 'close the sale'. This was the first time in their career that they had ever challenged that belief. The moment they did, it just fell apart.

The notion that the salesperson can close the sale is an illusion rather like the notion that you can win lotto. You can't close the sale and you can't win lotto. Note the active tense used here, it's very important. Neither can you win roulette, a horse race, or a vote. If you could win, in the active sense, you'd do it every time and you'd be the most famous person who ever lived.

The verb *to win*, when used in these examples in the active tense, is an illusion. A very costly illusion that has cost many a life, a fortune and a career. Nothing is better documented, every time there's a lotto draw, than the fact that you *cannot* win. Recently the nightly news showed millions of Americans lining up for hours to buy lotto tickets in a jackpot that was building to US$450 million. Presumably, they all wanted to win. Did they all win? No, they did not. The facts showed that over 99.9 per cent of all these people did not win – they were losers. If the focus was placed on this overwhelming piece of evidence then it would be clear that you can't win lotto. But the clever trick played by the lotto people is that they hide this fact by not mentioning the losers and spend a lot of money and media focusing on the so-called winner. This helps maintain the illusion for the faithful that, yes, you *can* win lotto. This clever trick of ignoring the losers is played on millions of willing players every day all around the world. Of course, most people get their value from the fantasy of winning for a few days before the bad news arrives. I'm one of them.

The illusion of winning is no less an illusion just because it's widely believed. If 10 million people are led to believe the earth is flat, that's not enough to make it flat. If 10 million salespeople are led to believe that they can close the sale, that's not enough to make it possible.

You can't win, in the active sense. Winning can only happen to you in the passive sense. It's a question of odds. In lotto, the odds against winning happening to you are very low, more than 1 million to 1.

In selling, the odds of winning happening to you are much better, often as high as 50/50. You win if the customer gives you a YES and you don't win if the customer gives you a NO.

If you, dear reader, can prove that you can close the sale and get only a YES, I'll give you $100,000. Please, email me at michael@newsellcoaching.com because you'll make me a very rich man. If you can show me how to make the customer say YES I could win a Nobel Prize for the scientific breakthrough of controlling the electrochemical behaviour of the human brain. But, more practically, I'd be on the first plane to New York to visit some of the largest companies in the world.

How much do you think they'd pay me for that sort of information?

4

Customers Detest Oldsell

Why do customers detest oldsell and why has oldsell produced such poor results – making a joke out of the selling profession into the bargain?

'Did you close the sale?'
– Sales Manager to Salesperson

Doctor of *Selling*?

In 1981, I was awarded the world's first PhD in Lateral Thinking. The degree, Doctor of Philosophy in Cognitive Science from the California State Department of Education, was for using lateral thinking to propose a new theory of selling. My tutor was the 'father of lateral thinking', Professor Edward de Bono, Director of the Cognitive Research Trust (CoRT) at Cambridge University in the UK. At the commencement of the project Professor de Bono wrote, 'Your application of the principles and attitudes of lateral thinking to selling in your NewSell approach is, to me, an interesting and powerful approach to an important area. What particularly interests me is your proposal to test theoretical constructs in a very practical manner in your field work.'

My external examiner was Professor George Gallup of the Gallup Poll at Princeton. He was the marketing giant who invented market research. On the successful completion of the newsell project (which ended up involving 40,000 employees at 24 New York City hospitals) Professor Gallup wrote, 'Newsell is the first new strategy for selling in 50 years! You have presented a new approach to a very old subject with proof that your ideas do work. I find some parallels in your thoughts about selling and my own views on how advertising works.'

To develop a new theory of selling, the first thing I had to do was to find out what the current or traditional theory of selling or salesmanship was all about. I had to look at the definitions of selling provided by various experts and the general view of selling that prevailed in the marketplace.

Definitions of Selling

Here were some experts' definitions of selling:

1. Selling is the process of determining the needs and wants of a prospective buyer and of presenting a product, service, or idea in such a way that a buyer is motivated to make a favourable buying decision. (John W. Ernest and Richard Ashmun, *Selling Principles and Practices* (New York: McGraw-Hill, 1979), p. 3).

2. Selling is the process of persuading or aiding the prospect in the purchasing of a product or service. (Gary Miller and C. Winston Borgen, *Professional Selling Inside and Out* (New York: Van Nostrand Reinhold, 1979), p. 12).

3. Salesmanship ... the art of persuading another person to do something when you do not have, or do not care to exert, the direct power to force the person to do it. (Fred A. Russell, Frank H. Beach, and Richard H. Buskirk, *Textbook of Salesmanship*, 10th ed. (New York: McGraw-Hill, 1978), p. 9).

4 Selling is the personal or impersonal process of assisting and/or persuading a prospective customer to buy a commodity or service, or to act favourably upon an idea that has commercial significance to the seller (The American Marketing Association, Definitions of Terms (Chicago, 1961), p. 7).

5 Salesmanship is defined as the process by which the salesman provides a buyer with maximum satisfaction by determining the buyer's needs for products or services and by persuading the buyer to purchase specific goods to fulfill these needs. Underlying this definition are two key elements: one, the buyer's need, and two, persuasion (N. Hampton and H. Zabin, *College Salesmanship* (New York: McGraw-Hill, 1958), p. 6).

6 Professional salesmanship ... may be defined as the process of analysing a buyer's need for a product or service, recommending the product or service that best satisfies the need, and persuading the buyer that the price is fair, the source of supply is satisfactory and now is the time to buy. (B.R. Canfield, *Salesmanship: Practices and Problems* (New York: McGraw-Hill, 1958), p. 6).

7 The selling process. The first step is to locate those who are, or should be most interested in what you have to offer (Leon Epstein, *Where Do You Go From No: Selling Simplified* (New York: Sales Research Institute, 1951), p. 5).

Customers' Opinions on Selling

In addition to the definitions of the experts, it was necessary to get the opinions of 'the person in the street': the customer. Since it's the individual members of the marketplace who are the target of our selling activities, their opinions provide a reflection of the current state of the art. Over a three-year period, different individuals and groups of individuals were asked to write down, in their own words, their opinion of the definition of selling or salesmanship. Among those given this proposal were sales managers, sales professionals, students, executives, technicians, interior designers, architects, artists, housewives, doctors, and others. The examples given here are typical of the responses:

1. Selling, according to my definition, implies the ability to convey all the necessary information in order to 'close the sale'. Through the use of total communication the salesman uses his techniques in order to persuade the customer to purchase his product, etc.

2. Selling – to give information about something which another might be interested in, actually 'closing a sale', collecting compensation for something which is going to another person.

3. Selling is persuading others to accept or purchase your product or service (or ideas).

4 Selling is getting people to buy (hopefully by ethical methods).

5 Selling is receiving money from someone for something they need that you have.

6 Selling has two meanings: (a) a specialised one – a retailer of goods, products; and (b) a generalised one – an individual who sells a concept.

7 Salesmanship is giving people what they want at the price they are willing to pay.

8 Selling – when you would like someone to try your product.

9 Selling – someone trying to give you something to make a profit.

10 Salesmanship – to persuade someone to buy a given product, especially when they are in doubt.

11 Selling – persuading someone to buy something they may or may not want.

Primary Observation: Close the sale

The definitions and opinions above show that selling is seen as something the salesperson *does* to the customer. Most participants thought that 'closing the sale' was the dominant idea in selling and they viewed the moment when ownership of the product was transferred to the prospect as the primary moment of selling. Their focus was always on the close, the destination or end result, rather than, say, the start, the journey or the process.

Examples: 'Getting people to buy'; 'persuading others'; 'giving people what they want'; 'determining the needs ... and presenting the product'; 'the process of persuading or aiding'; 'the art of persuading another'; 'determining the buyer's needs'; 'locate those interested'; 'the buyer is motivated to make a favourable buying decision'; 'the purchasing of a product'; 'another person to do something'; 'persuading others to accept or purchase your product'; 'getting people to buy'; 'actually closing a sale'; 'persuading someone to buy something.'

Selling is viewed as something you 'do' to someone to 'get' a result of some sort. The salesperson persuades the prospect and closes the sale.

Customers' Expectations

Customers have been taught to expect that it is the salesperson's goal to 'close the sale' in each selling situation. But this is not limited to customers. This expectation also appears to be the main environmental factor that exists in the sales organisation. During the past 25 years I have worked with thousands of salespeople, their trainers and their managers in the US, Europe, Asia and Australia. The clearest observation I have made is consistent everywhere. An expectation has been conditioned into:

- *sales managers* that their salespeople should 'close the sale'
- *salespeople* that they are expected to 'close the sale'
- *prospects* that the salesperson is going to try 'to close me'.

On numerous occasions I have asked individuals and groups the following: 'What is the first question a sales manager asks a salesperson returning from a sales call?' Invariably, the answer is: 'Did you close the sale?'

Currently, most salespeople work in an environment in which their sales managers expect that they should always 'close the sale'. This expectation is then projected onto the customer who thinks, 'he's trying to close me'. In addition, the method (well understood by the experts, sales managers, salespeople and the public alike) will use some form of persuasion or exhortation. Sales books, training courses, direct-marketing schemes and television commercials reinforce the customer view and educate the sales force that selling involves some form of exhortation that the prospects 'should buy something'.

Exhortation and Pressure

In my research I was unable to find any sales training course, whether in books, on cassettes, or in seminar form, that did not teach 'closing the sale' as the primary focus. This means that each of these approaches involves exhortation to either a greater or lesser degree. Sometimes the courses make a distinction between high and low pressure, but usually pressure is the method or technique they are teaching.

The Theory of Selling

The current theory of selling is the same as that which existed 80 years ago when the subject began to be formally written about. The traditional view is that salespeople should sell their prospects in order to get the sale.

The Current Theory of Selling:

The Salesperson Closes the Sale

This means that the salespeople 'do' something to their prospects. This usually involves persuasion, high or low pressure, or some other form of exhortation that the prospects buy . . . now!

The current theory of selling produces an expectation on the part of:

- *sales managers* that their salespeople close the sale
- *salespeople* that they should always close the sale
- *prospects* that the salesperson will try to close me.

A lot of the existing material written for the training of salespeople has a mystical or metaphysical spin. Indeed many of the authors of these programs are also religious preachers from the US, men like Zig Ziglar and Reverend Robert Schuller.

In my opinion, one of the reasons why there's so much exhortation, pressure and judgmentalism in selling practices is because of the old-fashioned 'convert the sinner' and 'close the sale' attitudes. All this preaching and evangelising is a turn-off. Perhaps this is why selling is held in such low-esteem by customers. The customer will be better served if there is more science in selling.

Business + Science

Is there is room for science in selling? I think there is and I also think that there is an opportunity for a greater synthesis of the attitudes of the global business world with the organised mental techniques, mensuration and testing we use in science.

Business is a wonderful laboratory. Every business is an experiment in how to make a profit. Every business day provides an opportunity for a fresh start. With its highly measurable bottom line, business is an ideal setting for the scientific attitude. Science, too, can learn a lot from the pragmatism and flexibility of the business attitude. In other words, I would like to see more science in business and more business in science.

What is science?

Scientific theories are essentially different to religious theories in one way. Scientific theories are fallible. They are made to be challenged, dismantled and reconstructed whenever they are proved to be factually wrong. They embrace change. The amazing march of science in the past 300 years is a testimony to this feature of fallibility. Science never wants to discover the 'best' truth, but rather a better one than the one we have at present.

On the other hand, religious theories are made to be 'absolute truth'. Because they are based not on fact but on belief, through subjective inspiration, they are the absolute or best truth and, since best cannot be improved upon, they are defended against change. This feature kicked off the second millennium with the brutal religious wars of the crusades, a fight which has continued for a thousand years.

In religious theory, for example, an assertion is made: 'This is what Jesus said. Trust us because it's the absolute truth.' As a result, thinking is then directed towards defending that position from change since 'absolute truth' cannot be made better.

In science theory, a different approach is taken. The question is asked, 'Yes, but what did Jesus *really* say?' Then the questioning attitudes and techniques of scholarship supported by the search for hard evidence are used to uncover a better understanding of the 'more likely' sayings of Jesus. The process continues, never reaching the *best* truth but always reaching a *better* truth.

The same applies to selling. It is not enough to believe that a salesperson closes the sale. In science, we need proof that this is possible. I'll address this further later in this book.

The Synthetic Millennium

As you read this, don't forget that you are living in a world where the human species is on the verge of decommissioning natural selection and designing its own future. As we said goodbye to the 'Mystical Millennium' we learned how to explain to ourselves by darwinian evolution how our species came to be and why it is the way it is. At the end of the old millennium, we found geneticists busily mapping out the entire human genetic code, the detailed DNA blueprint for the programming of our species. Just imagine what this now means!

In the Synthetic Millennium, we see the human species about to switch from darwinian to 'volitional' evolution. We'll soon be designing our genes for volitional selection to choose how we want our species to evolve. Will we choose to enhance traits like intelligence, height or manual dexterity or will we choose to diversify our talents and pluralise our temperaments? We'll soon need to make some very difficult decisions of the Faustian variety. The American biologist, Edward O. Wilson, puts the question this way: 'How much should people be allowed to mutate themselves and their descendants?'

Choices, choices, choices

The Synthetic Millennium will be characterised by choice. Not only will we be choosing the future design of our species but, on a daily basis, buyers will be called upon to make more and more choices than ever before. The time has come to take a serious, scientific approach to the important business of selling.

What is Selling?

Why is selling like leadership or treason?

Selling is an art but it can be a science

As you have no doubt guessed, the focus of newsell is the customer. That is why it's called 'new'. Before newsell the focus was the salesperson. In working with business people over three generations around the world, my observation has been that the change from salesperson-focus to customer-focus is a very big change of mindset which only a small minority of salespeople, entrepreneurs, sales managers and CEOs have yet been able to make.

From the customer's viewpoint, selling can sometimes seem like leadership when a problem has been solved in a satisfactory way or when a new opportunity has been created for his or her benefit. This is the classic win/win scenario. But when the customer has been used, abused or betrayed, then selling can seem like treachery. Even if this is an 'I-win-you-lose' situation for the salesperson in the short term, in today's global marketplace it's a lose/lose scenario for the brand in the longer term.

But what *is* selling?

Before he died, my friend and mentor Fred Herman wrote a book called *Selling Is Simple* (New York: Vantage, 1979) and was the co-author with Earl Nightingale of the *KISS program: Keep It Simple, Salesman*. Earl Nightingale used to say that Fred Herman was 'America's Greatest Sales Trainer' and Fred used to say, 'Selling is simple, it just isn't easy!'.

I would agree with Fred. However, like most other subjects, much has been done by the experts to complicate the issue of selling and salesmanship. It can be difficult for someone to ever find out just what the fundamental point about selling actually is.

If you wish, stop here for a moment and ask yourself this question: 'If I were asked to choose the one word that best covers the fundamental process of selling, what word would that be?' Before going on, you can write your word here: _____ (This isn't a test, just an opportunity for you to do some thinking.)

I think selling is nothing more than trying to achieve a change in someone's behaviour – yours, mine, or theirs.

Change

- You try to sell yourself on giving up smoking.
- She tries to sell herself on losing weight.
- I try to sell myself on learning Spanish.
- Mother tries to sell her son on eating his vegetables.
- Teachers try to sell their students on doing their homework.
- Employers try to sell their employees on increasing productivity.
- Your sales manager tries to sell you on making more calls.
- Agents try to sell their prospects to buying more insurance.
- Politicians try to sell their constituencies on turning out to vote.

What is the fundamental process here? It is change. Selling is a process. Selling is the process of changing behaviour. Can you think of any exception to this? To elaborate, we can say that selling is the process of changing the current state of behaviour to a better state of behaviour. 'Better', of course, is defined by the one carrying out the process – the salesperson.

The Concept of Change

To understand selling we must first understand the binary concept of change, which is one of the simplest of all concepts. If there is a minimum of two states, then there exists the possibility of moving from one state to the other – the possibility of change. The concept of change also includes the concept of escape. In order to move to a different state we have to escape from the current state.

So, for example, we can move or escape:

- from hot to cold = change
- from up to down = change
- from black to white = change
- from before to after = change
- from current to better = change
- from flip to flop = change
- from UNCHECK to CHECK = change.

Alternatives

To change behaviour (which is the object of selling), again, there must be a minimum of two states. There must be an alternative state to the one we are currently in. In other words, if we could not imagine any alternative to our current behaviour, then we could have no basis for change. A prerequisite for a change in current behaviour (mine, yours, or theirs) must be the feasibility of at least one alternative state of behaviour.

Selling: Before and After

Selling is what happens between 'before' and 'after'. Before selling we have one state of behaviour. After selling we have another state of behaviour. It is selling or salesmanship that affects the change.

In real life, selling is that which is required to change current behaviour to better behaviour. It is the need for the positive upgrading of the situation from its current state to a better state that produces the need for selling. Anyone who is sincerely interested in improving situations, in quality, is interested in selling.

What Is 'Better'?

If selling is upgrading current behaviour to better behaviour, who decides what is 'better' behaviour? This is really the most important point in this discussion on selling and the one which always has caused the most confusion.

I have already said, 'Better, of course, is defined by the one carrying out the process – the salesperson.' Do you agree? Think about this point for a moment and write 'yes' or 'no' in this space _____.

I was wrong. The correct answer is 'NO! NO! NO!'

In selling, 'better' is defined by the prospect, not by the salesperson. For prospects to change their current behaviour to a better behaviour, the new behaviour must be better from the prospect's point of view! This is where most mistakes take place in selling.

The only time it matters what you think is better is when it is your behaviour that is being changed. If you want to change my current behaviour to better behaviour, then it must be better from my point of view.

The average person is more concerned about him- or herself than about the ten most famous people who ever lived. This is the natural state of things and there doesn't appear to be any evidence that it is going to change. Until we recognise this, there's little we can do to influence the behaviour of individuals and groups of individuals or even nations of individuals.

When you want to change behaviour from its current state to a better state, be sure 'better' is defined by your prospect. 'Better' is in the eye of the beholder!

Thinking, Selling and Leadership

The discussion above applies to leadership, which is a special application of selling, or vice versa. Leadership is the skill of getting others to lead themselves. So is selling or salesmanship. Like all skills, leadership/salesmanship can be learned. How? By acquiring the lateral thinking skill of generating better alternatives so attractive to other people that they will want to make a positive change in their behaviour.

Selling is leadership in a commercial context and leadership is selling in a social context.

The Failure of Sales Training

Why do salespeople *without* sales trainers often do better than salespeople *with* sales trainers?

How good are we at sales training? Unfortunately for most of us, the answer is 'Not very!' In fact, we are very, very poor at sales training. It is a well-documented fact that in the US a mere *20 per cent* of salespeople account for *80 per cent* of the nation's gross sales. The results are about the same in Australia. Although this is well known in the sales profession, the American economy still spends billions of dollars annually hiring, training, subsidising, and finally replacing salespeople, and then it starts all over again.

In 1996 in the US, just before the Internet revolution, sales executives spent over US$5 billion in the process of locating and training sales personnel. More than US$12 billion was spent in just the direct costs (advertising, executive time, testing, instructing) involved in finding, training and then losing sales people. At least 25 per cent of recruits changed jobs during the first year and a staggering proportion of the remaining 70 per cent lost sales, burned territories and were destined to change jobs before the end of the second year.

Back in the 1920s, the insurance industry funded an intensive project to address this costly agent turnover, which stood at more than 65 per cent in the first year and up to 85 per cent in the first three years. Measured again 70 years later, turnover of agents in the insurance industry was still 65 per cent in the first year and 85 per cent in the first three years.

In the last 70 years, billions of dollars have been spent on teaching oldsell methods to salespeople. Never before have there been so many training and motivation courses covering things like sales analysis, psychoanalysis, transactional analysis, closing techniques, objection handlers, reverse selling, positive thinking and so forth, in the form of books, tapes and CDs, films and DVDs, seminars, incentive programs, conferences and camps.

There are commissions, prizes and bonuses and trips and contests and conventions. Yet the situation has not improved even one percentage point!

Consider the astonishing cost to shareholders of the failure of sales training. The waste of company resources, time, money and energy spent on recruiting, testing, selecting, training and supervising salespeople each year, only to start over again the next year. Imagine if this happened in the other professions!

Yet, this is nothing compared to the cost to the economy in lack of productivity or the human costs in 'psychic currency': missed opportunities, burnt territories, customer disservice, tarnished company reputations, poor morale and the stigma of failure. Perhaps the time has come to step back and take an objective look at the situation.

The Failure of Sales Training

The breathtaking failure of sales training is one of the legendary business phenomena of our time. When compared to other managements, sales managements around the world have demonstrated a poor level of professional competence in this critical area. In fact, a management that regularly turns over 80 per cent of its workforce can hardly be considered management at all! If an investigative journalist team examined the sales industry at management level, they would uncover the greatest business scandal since the beginning of the Industrial Revolution.

Marketplace Distrust of Sales Profession

In 1980, George Gallup told me that in the annual Gallup Poll on honesty and ethics, which asked the US marketplace to rate 24 professions and occupations on whether 'the honesty and ethical standards' of those in the field were from 'very high' to 'very low', the five worst professions were:

20 labor leaders
21 state officeholders
22 insurance salespeople
23 advertising practitioners
24 car salespeople.

Here's a profession that cannot even sell itself to the public so it's no surprise that its failure to sell its products and services has been so massive.

In the 2005 Gallup survey of honesty and ethics, firefighters topped the list, followed by nurses and members of the military in second and third places. Pharmacists, medical doctors and the clergy also received high marks. The biggest change was in the higher ratings received by the police, up 13 percentage points from the previous year. Car salesmen come in last, as they have for the past two and a half decades.

The Blaming of Salespeople

What is sad about this state of affairs is that sales managements have passed the buck onto their employees. Sales managers have behaved as though the conditions described here are the fault of the salespeople, when clearly they are the responsibilities of management.

For example, think of the number of sincere, enthusiastic young people who have been thrilled at their successful hiring and graduation from sales class. Trustingly putting their futures in the hands of incompetent sales managements, they have gone out into the field into hopeless selling situations that no experienced professional would ever dream of taking on. Failing (of course), they have been allowed – even encouraged – to think it was their fault. Meanwhile, management has already placed the advertisement for the next batch of sincere, enthusiastic young people ... Believe it or not, this situation is still considered 'normal' by many sales managements in the insurance industry. They dispassionately call it 'agent turnover'.

The Selling Profession

The economy needs competent sales management, since the selling profession is the back on which the economy rides. As a profession, it is principally responsible for the standard of living of the rest of the nation. Although, in a modern society, selling is easily as important a profession as the law, medicine, the church, science or the arts, the community scarcely perceives it that way. For this we pay a price we can ill afford.

In a Woody Allen movie, the ultimate punishment in prison if you misbehaved was to be locked up in isolation ... with an insurance salesman! Judging by the audience's laughter, there were few who did not appreciate the joke.

Strategically, it never will be possible to change those 20/80 percentages until we do something to change the way the customer-base feels about the selling profession. This responsibility falls squarely on the shoulders of current and future sales managements.

Rejection and Reluctance

One of the biggest causes for the failure of salespeople is rejection. I once saw a survey on the habits of salespeople which showed 'call reluctance' as the major area requiring the attention of sales management.

So sales managers tell their people, 'Make calls! You gotta make more calls!'

Yet anyone who is in selling already knows he or she has to make calls; so what really is the problem here? The real killer-blow of rejection is delivered to the salesperson by his own sales manager when he or she returns to the office. What does the sales manager say?

'DID YOU GET THE SALE?' (I call this DYSHing the salesperson – DYSH – **D**id **Y**ou **S**ell **H**im/**H**er?).

'Er, not exactly, you see what happened was this, ah ...' and the salesperson really feels like a jerk. As a consequence, one common way salespeople avoid the rejection they feel when their sales managers DYSH them is this – they don't make any calls.

No calls means, of course, they're out of business. Dead. Killed by their own sales manager's 'Did-you-get-the-sale?' preoccupation with results. So often we have found that salespeople *with* sales managers perform less productively than salespeople *without* sales managers. The only justification for the existence of a sales manager is the degree of service he or she provides to his or her salespeople. Mere scorekeeping is not the same as serving.

No Villains

To be fair, there are really no villains here. Salesperson abuse is like child abuse, it's often hereditary. The reason so many sales managers abuse their salespeople is because they, themselves, were abused by their sales managers and it's just been handed down from generation to generation. But the opportunity now exists for a new generation of sales managers to break the chain and to switch from DYSHing their salespeople to serving them as they would have their salespeople serve their customers.

Management is Service

If the sales manager is not serving the customer then he or she had better be serving someone who is! Serving salespeople is the role of the professional sales manager. Here's what others have to say about the leader as servant:

KING GEORGE VI
The highest of distinctions is service to others.

MARK 10:44
And whosoever of you will be the chiefest,
shall be the servant of all.

MALCOMN S. FORBES
Everybody has to be somebody to somebody
to be anybody.

MATTHEW 23:12
For whoever exalts himself will be humbled, and
whoever humbles himself will be exalted.

JOHN FLORIO
Who has not served cannot command.

ALBERT EINSTEIN
The high destiny of the individual is to serve
rather than to rule.

A New Way of Selling

We have already discussed the insurance industry's problems with agent turnover. To varying degrees, this problem affects the whole of the selling profession, which suffers more job losses than any other industry group. Sales managements spend more time recruiting, training, DYSHing and losing salespeople than they do serving them.

What if there were a better alternative to oldsell? What would happen to rejection? What would happen to call reluctance? What would happen to the turnover of salespeople? What would happen to the recruiting problem? How would customers feel about a salesperson? What would be the image of salespeople and the prestige of the profession? What would happen to salesman's jokes?

There *is* a better alternative. It's a new way of selling. I call it newsell.

7

TCB: Taking Care of Business

Why is 'taking care of business' more profitable than 'closing the sale'?

If oldsell is the problem, let's look at the solution. But before going onto newsell in Part Two, experience has shown me that we should take a moment to talk about the 'closing the sale' issue. Newsell is simple, but some people's brains, infected with oldsell, can have real difficulty when they first hear about it. The oldsell virus may be so strong that they just cannot imagine any alternative to 'closing the sale'.

So, to help clarify it I ask these people the following question, 'Do you always get a YES from your customers?' They admit that they don't always get YES, often they get NO. In other words, they get a mixture of responses from their customers, a mixture of YES and NO decisions. Yet, even though they know, from their own experience, that they really don't control the customer's buying decision, they still cannot see what could possibly take the place of 'closing the sale'.

There are two comments to make here:

1 Just because one cannot imagine an alternative to 'closing the sale' does not mean that such an alternative cannot exist. It may simply be a failure of imagination.

2 If 'closing the sale' is a bad idea, the fact that a lot of people believe in it is not enough to make it a good idea. There are those who believe snake handling is a good enough idea to pass it on to their children. But that doesn't mean it is.

The reason for newsell is because oldsell has failed us. Our confidence in oldsell is misplaced. If oldsell did work then I could still offer newsell as an alternative but one might say, 'Why bother changing when the current sales strategy works so well?' ... but it doesn't! Eighty per cent of the nation's gross sales in 2005 were still made by only 20 per cent of the sales force.

There has been more nonsense written about selling than in any other area of business. Each year, Australian companies spend many millions on corporate sales meetings, corporate sales training, sales seminars, sales training collaterals, sales incentives and other sales development expenses. Unfortunately, very little change in the 80/20 situation is derived from these massive corporate expenditures.

The facts prove that most of what is promoted as 'sales training' is pure old-fashioned nonsense. Well meaning, perhaps, but nonsense just the same.

If we are to change all this in the new millennium we have to admit that our traditional theory of selling has been crude and primitive, inadequate and expensive, and sometimes dangerous and destructive.

The high costs of creeping overheads, the ever-competitive market and the chaotic economic environment demand that a serious, credible and scientific approach be given to the basic business strategy of selling. Few companies can continue to afford the missed sales opportunities and lost profits caused by archaic sales doctrine and hardened thinking patterns.

TCB

We can wrap up this Part One discussion on The Close with a simple answer to the question: What is an alternative to The Close?

Answer: The TCB.

The TCB stands for Taking Care of Business and we all do it quite naturally all the time. Daily human commerce is all about taking care of business. We are all familiar with making decisions, choosing amounts, considering options, refusing or accepting offers, listening to propositions, seeking advice, thinking things over, changing our minds, acting on impulse and so on. We've all done these things so many times. This is the normal daily taking care of business or TCB. You simply ask a question and you get a response:

TCB – What time is it? ... It's just turned noon.

TCB – Would you pass me the sugar? ... Sure, here it is.

TCB – Which way to the nearest bus stop? ... Sorry, I'm from out of town.

TCB – Do you want to go to the movies tonight? ... No thanks, I've got to study.

TCB – Tea or coffee? ... Just a glass of water, please.

TCB – How will you pay for this? ... I think I'll use my Amex card.

TCB – Here are the contracts. ... Thanks, I'll give them to my lawyer.

TCB – Do you need anything else today? ... No, but can you help me to the car?

TCB – Press the SEND button on the screen for your e-commerce cybertransaction.

TCB – Mate, can you spare me twenty cents? ... Here's a dollar.

TCB – Would you like to be considered for an invitation? ... Yes, please.

TCB – Do you want to bring a guest? ... Let me think who. I'll call you back.

TCB – Would you like our How To Vote card? ... No thanks.

TCB – Take a number and join the queue. ... No, I'll go next door.

TCB – We've got some new stock in, do you want to take a look? ... Yes, but not now. I'll come back later.

Whenever, as a customer, our attention is drawn to an offer, we respond by taking care of business. This may involve refusing the offer or accepting the offer, a simple YES or NO. It may involve negotiating over terms or seeking further advice. We might get competitive quotes or take time to think it over. The timing might be good now or better next month. All of this is normal TCB, taking care of business. With or without closing techniques we do what we want.

Whenever, as a customer, an offer is presented to us we TCB. But the key point here is this:

It's not The Close
that gives us the opportunity to TCB
it's The Start.

2

The Start
AND
The Newsell
Strategy

The Start

'It's not the *close* that takes care of business,
it's the *start*.

CVS to BVS

CVS to BVS is what I call a thinking switch. It means that
the current view of the situation (CVS) can never be equal
to the better view of the situation (BVS). I have written in
more detail about CVS to BVS in *Software for Your Brain*
which you can download for free at:

www.schoolofthinking.org/downloads/brainsoftware.pdf

Back when Jack Welch was Chairman of General Electric, he
called me once and left an urgent message on my
voicemail: 'Michael, I need a BVS!' GE was in crisis. Caspar
Weinberger, the then US Secretary of Defence, had
cancelled the company's defence contracts. This was a
direct and immediate threat to a brand which at the time
appeared on everything in American homes from light

bulbs to refrigerators. Jack went on to use a CVS to BVS strategy throughout the General Electric Company. 'Finding a better way every day' became a GE slogan which was put up in every GE office and factory around the world. He used the CVS to BVS idea to create a new strategy for GE which he called *boundarylessness*. The idea kept spreading and evolving and today the Ford Motor Company use the slogan 'No Boundaries' in their TV commercials. This is just one example of the power of the CVS to BVS idea.

In the next few chapters I'll show you how Jack used my formula CVS X10 = BVS to help him bring GE back from the brink. He went on to grow GE from a $35-billion manufacturing company to an empire worth more than $350 billion.

I'd like first to draw your attention to the paradox of starting. Once you get started there is momentum and feedback but getting started can be difficult. The paradox of starting is this: most races are lost not at the finishing line but at the starting blocks. Why? Because most people never even enter the race! They just never get started.

At the Beijing Olympics in 2008 only one swimmer will win the gold medal for the men's 400-metres freestyle. Before the race, there will be a dozen or more swimmers on the starting blocks pumped and ready to go. Thousands will witness this exciting event in 'The Water Cube', Beijing's spectacular new National Swimming Center, and several billion global viewers will watch it on a screen. But even on that day, most people on the planet will just not get started.

The Start of the Sale = Customer Attention

The start of the sale is customer attention. Before a customer can say YES or NO their attention must be on your offer. Fred Herman, author of *KISS: Keep It Simple Salesman*, used to say, 'First, you've got to get the customer's attention.' Yet, most of the time the vast majority of customers' attention is not focused on your offer at all, and when the customer's attention is not on your offer then there can be no hope of a sale.

The Check Move

To manage customer attention I designed a new unit of measurement which I called the Check move. A Check move (taken from the game of chess) is simply a customer contact of any kind and is represented by the symbol: C

For years it's been a common belief in selling that most sales were lost at the close. In other words, salespeople were missing sales because they were not 'closing' them. Our research showed that this simply isn't true. The whole issue of 'closing the sale' is a nonsense and I have offered a reward of $100,000 to the first person who can prove the salesperson closes the sale.

FACT: The decision to buy is an electro-chemical event in the brain of the customer and the salesperson does NOT control that event.

FACT: 99 per cent of sales are not missed at the close at all but at the start.

FACT: It's the failure to start the sale – to contact a customer by phone, by snail mail, by email, by fax or in person – that is the source of most lost business.

FACT: 99 per cent of C moves haven't even been made.

Keeping track of their C moves (customer contacts) helps salespeople measure how much energy they are putting out into the marketplace. Focusing on their C moves helps them:

1 raise their energy level and avoid wasting time
2 stop their obsession with 'the close' and all the archaic manipulation tactics that customers hate and which have given the selling profession such a bad name.

Focusing on the start – C – rather than 'the close', reduces the rejection and disappointment salespeople feel and boosts their energy levels. C allows them to initiate many more customer contacts.

This, of course, leads to better sales results because the only move that can turn a prospective customer into a client is CHECK which is enough to make it the most important move in business. As Woody Allen once said, 'Eighty per cent of success is showing up.'

MBO or MBS?

Most plans in life are full of details on how to get to the finishing line but contain little or nothing about how to get to the starting blocks. Yet nothing happens until someone STARTS something.

For many years in business we have had MBO or 'Management By Objectives'. We also need MBS or 'Management By Starting'.

Many management gurus write books about 'Goal-Setting'. Maybe they should also write books about 'Start-Getting' since, most of the time, most people never get started.

To start is the fundamental creative act. To change a switch from the OFF position to the ON position is to start something and means something has now been created. It has been said that the most important skill in writing a book is sitting down at the keyboard – getting started.

Strategy is all about control. If you are in control you are in a strategic position, if you are out of control, you aren't. Starting is a strategic act because we can control it but we cannot control finishing.

Once we start, many other factors come into play: other people's reactions, the weather, consequences and the unexpected. These may prevent us from finishing. But if we are good at starting then we can always start again, and again, and again. It may be that finishing is simply the repetitive act of starting, and starting again, and starting again, until we declare that we have 'finished'.

There is a southern American expression called 'the get-go' which I really like. The get-go is the start, the beginning, the very first step. In oldsell, most sales are lost right from the get-go because, the sale never got started.

The Physics of Selling

I designed newsell for people in business, whether in a Fortune 500 corporation or a small family company. Perhaps you are in business for yourself at home, in a small office, in a partnership or joint-venture. Or maybe you are an MLMer or a salesperson on salary or commission. Or you may be just contemplating exploring some of these business opportunities. Whatever the case, newsell will help you understand the physics of selling and allow you to develop the basic skills of doing business professionally and successfully.

What do I mean by the physics of selling? In short, you have two things in selling physics to work with: TIME and ENERGY. Every customer contact, every time you move from UNCHECK to CHECK, requires a unit of TIME + ENERGY.

In the next few chapters we'll look at these two basic resources – TIME + ENERGY – and give you:

1 a new unit of measurement for managing your energy more productively and
2 a new strategy for expanding your time called 'cybertime'. Cybertime is a new way for you to get a better appreciation of time as a resource.

Newsell is young, fast and scientific. With newsell, we are only interested in control – methods that can be tested or results that can be measured. Newsell is not interested in academic, philosophical or motivational hype. These can be found elsewhere. Newsell focuses on building the field power of the businessperson. The field power comes from his/her two fundamental assets: time and energy. In military terms, this is called 'force'. Logistically speaking, results are directly linked to how well you can apply this force, this field power, to the marketplace. The more force (time and energy), the more results.

NOTE: The use of the word 'force' refers to logistics here. It does not refer to style. It is not the style that is forceful: that would be oldsell. It's the big increase of time and energy in the marketplace that is forceful, as we shall see.

Using the newsell strategy maximises your fundamental assets in the field by:

- increasing activity and
- reducing fatigue.

Force

Force has its limitations – there are only 168 hours in a week and there is a limit to how much energy one can exert. But most of us aren't coming close to challenging those limitations. If we are going to find extra force and to reallocate it to sales and business activity it has to come from somewhere.

But where do we find this extra field power, this extra force? In oldsell, considerable time and energy was used up by 'the close' even though, as we have seen, the salesperson cannot control 'the close'. So we can take back the time and energy lost doing the oldsell dance called 'the close of the sale'.

Example: A company sent out a seminar invitation to accountants. They followed up with telephone calls of the oldsell variety nervously asking, 'Would you please come to our seminar?' After two weeks they had only two positive responses and were understandably disappointed with the results. Then someone in the company suggested a newsell approach. They sent out another letter with a chocolate Freddo Frog and made follow-up phonecalls of the newsell variety asking, 'Did you get your Freddo Frog?' This time they got 32 seminar attendees.

Focusing on the close makes both the salesperson and the customer nervous and wastes precious energy. It also makes salespeople reluctant to make more calls. Focusing on the process (Did you get the frog?) is much easier on both the salesperson and the customer and so more energy is available for more calls. More calls = more YES answers.

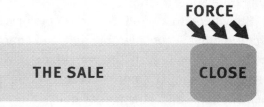

FORCE

THE SALE

CLOSE

OLDSELL

Oldsell is results-driven. The strategy is to focus on the close and that is where most of the force is squandered. Sales statistics show that this approach has failed. One of the main reasons for the failure is the lack of control. The decision to buy is controlled by the customer so any force applied to this area is a waste of field power.

The Theory of Newsell: The Customer Closes the Sale

Newsell is process-driven. The strategy is to remove the force being used up by the close and make it available for the area you can control – the start. The start is the customer contact, the actual making of the sales call, the process of selling. In newsell, we call the process the CHECK move or C.

The natural enemy of the businessperson is not the customer but fatigue. This fatigue is caused by trying to do the impossible, trying to close the sale. This wastes a huge amount of sales power and leads to call reluctance and lost sales.

Control the Process

You cannot control the result because you cannot control the customer's brain but you *can* control the selling process which is the customer contact. Newsell helps you avoid the principal cause of fatigue in selling – rejection – by giving you a selling strategy which puts you in control of the selling process.

> **Example:** A business development plan to increase the number of their clients who had access to the Internet was run by a financial services company. The plan was results-driven. The report stated: 'We have spoken to everyone and they don't want it.' A newsell-trained manager then ran a newsell 60-day campaign that focused salespeople on the process, not the results, of their offer. The result: An increase in new sites from 111 to 478 – more than 400 per cent!

We can control the process but we cannot control the result. Failure to understand this basic law of physics is the principal cause of failure amongst sales managers ... and losing salespeople is failure.

Time

How to create more time in business

> 'Time is money.'
> – Francis Bacon

In contrast to the military, the arts and sport, precious little time is devoted to skill training in business. I think this accounts for much of the shortfall in business skills. Of the small amount of time that is made available, most of it is spent on *knowledge* transference rather than *skill* transference. There are meetings and PowerPoint presentations and pep talks and even the odd 'bonding exercise'. Rarely, if ever, do business trainers focus on virtuosity.

When an hour is made available for training in the military, dojo, ballet studio or music conservatory, the focus will be on skill transference. This means 10 or 15 minutes might be devoted to content, to a 'lecture' or discussion, and 45 minutes will be devoted to practise, repetition and rehearsal. The mantra is simple: no drill no skill.

Selling, leadership and thinking are all skills. Without drills and rehearsals there is nothing left but warm feelings, motivational highs and passionate discourse. In my experience, this accounts for a lot of the failures in business.

In developing the intellectual capital of a profit-making enterprise, management must be continually finding ways to keep the attention of the enterprise focused on the two cardinal profit-making activities:

1 cutting costs and

2 raising revenues.

Management must provide simple, functional tools for their employees to manage these two activities in their own workspace. Knowledge-workers must be given training and a chance to practise these two fundamental business skills.

Newsell is a revenue-raising skill that everyone in business can develop as part of their intellectual capital. Newsell will help you acquire and refine the basic skills of doing business professionally and successfully without offending your customers.

Newsell Physics: TIME

The success of newsell comes from how it exploits the fundamental physics available to all business people – TIME and ENERGY.

Between the past and the future lies the only moment of time you can control ... the present. The present is that unique moment in time when the future becomes the past. In order to spend time you need to be able to control time, and the only moment for spending time is called ... Now!

Modern physics tells us that there is always an unlimited number of possible futures coming towards and at each particular moment. We 'choose' one of those futures ... Now!... and that selected future then becomes the unalterable past. Now! is the moment in time when the future becomes the past.

Measuring things is one way of controlling them. Units of measurement enable us to better manipulate things to our useful advantage. For example, kilometres enable us to control distances, kilometres per hour enable us to control speed, days help us to control time. With units of measurement, the smaller the unit the greater degree of control. So, we come to the concept of what I call 'Cybertime 24/7': the shift from measuring time in days to measuring it in hours.

In a week there are seven days and we know them by their individual names (the names are another form of measurement). These days are familiar and useful chunks of time. Their only disadvantage in spending them is their size. A day is so large and bulky, it can be quite cumbersome to spend. We lose patience, or interest. We get tired, distracted or bored.

If only we had an easier method of controlling time, of spending time ...

Cybertime 24/7

Cybertime 24/7 makes this possible by giving each hour its own name just as each day has its own name. Suddenly a certain hour is important because it is unique. It has its own name and cannot be confused with any other hour. Just as Monday is a unique day and never gets confused with Friday, in Cybertime 24/7 a certain hour never need be confused with another hour. Each hour can be planned and spent in its own way. So what shall we call these unique hours of time? What names shall we give them?

Since there are only 168 hours each and every week, why don't we (just for convenience) give each hour its own unique number. That way we can identify each hour as a special unit of time and be free to spend it as we please.

In the Cybertime map, Monday goes from Cybertime 1 to 24. Tuesday is Cybertime 25 to 48. Wednesday is Cybertime 49 to 72 and so on.

1	25	49	73	97	121	145
2	26	50	74	98	122	146
3	27	51	75	99	123	147
4	28	52	76	100	124	148
5	29	53	77	101	125	149
6	30	54	78	102	126	150
7	31	55	79	103	127	151
8	32	56	80	104	128	152
9	33	57	81	105	129	153
10	34	58	82	106	130	154
11	35	59	83	107	131	155
12	36	60	84	108	132	156
13	37	61	85	109	133	157
14	38	62	86	110	134	158
15	39	63	87	111	135	159
16	40	64	88	112	136	160
17	41	65	89	113	137	161
18	42	66	90	114	138	162
19	43	67	91	115	139	163
20	44	68	92	116	140	164
21	45	69	93	117	141	165
22	46	70	94	118	142	166
23	47	71	95	119	143	167
24	48	72	96	120	144	168

Spending Cybertime

Each of us gets a fresh deposit of 168 hours in our personal Cybertime account each week. We can either spend it ourselves or others will spend it for us. Because Cybertime is measured in hours, it is more flexible, more manageable and easier to spend. You can budget Cybertime just like you budget your cash flow. You can plan Cybertime for work, for health, for family, for friends, for yourself, for training, for entertainment, for maintenance, for fun, or for nothing! The main point is to spend it *yourself*.

Cybertime 24/7 is that point in time and space where one of the possible futures collapses into the actual past ... try to be there when it happens!

Energy

How to put more energy into business

'To be or not to be? That is the question.'
– William Shakespeare

As discussed in the previous chapter, the success of newsell comes from understanding the physics of business and how to exploit the two fundamental resources available to all businesspeople – TIME and ENERGY.

Energy is the second focus of the newsell physics.

A switch is a device for change. It is a mechanism for changing from one condition or state to another state. From OFF to ON, from FLIP to FLOP, from UP to DOWN, from LEFT to RIGHT, from IN to OUT, from CVS to BVS and so on. A switch is also a device for escape. With a switch one can escape from OFF, from FLIP, from UP, from LEFT, from IN and from a CVS.

Even the darkest room can be transformed into a blaze of living colours with the simple flick of a switch. We will show you how to use the newsell switch as a simple tool to allow you to escape from inertia and better control the other fundamental business resource, your energy.

The Newsell Switch

The newsell switch is designed in the form of a powerful piece of software for your brain to help you organise, in a strategic way, the simple but fundamental physics of all business transactions. The brain software is UNCHECKTOCHECK which is the way we write the switch – from UNCHECK to CHECK.

In any business transaction there are three basic situations: CHECKMATE, CHECK and UNCHECK.

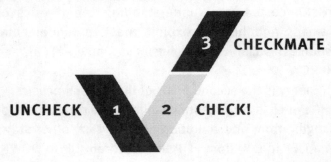

3 CHECKMATE

UNCHECK **1** **2** CHECK!

CHECKMATE

Above the Strategy Switch is CHECKMATE – the situation which signifies victory! In business, CHECKMATE is when the customer says YES.

CHECKMATE is known traditionally in selling as 'the close'. CHECKMATE is a decision which takes place in the brain of another person so that decision, by definition, is outside your control. This is a fact of scientific reality, the acknowledgment of which is a fundamental principle of newsell. To restate the theory of newsell: the customer closes the sale.

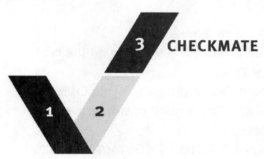

CHECKMATE is when a customer signs the order form, or when a buyer accepts the deal. In show business, it's when you get the part you auditioned for. For writers, it's when you sign the contract with the publisher. In sports, CHECKMATE is the moment when you get selected for the team.

The main strategic feature of the CHECKMATE situation is: the salesperson cannot control it.

CHECK

The situation just below CHECKMATE is when the switch is turned ON and is in the Right (as opposed to the Left) position. This is called CHECK.

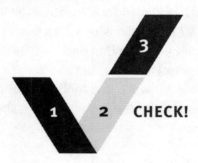

- CHECK is when it is possible for the customer to say NO or YES.
- Without CHECK there can be no CHECKMATE.
- CHECK is simply another word for 'customer contact'.
- CHECK = CUSTOMER CONTACT = CHECK
- CHECK is the penultimate state, the set-up move for CHECKMATE.
- CHECK is the position of the newsell switch which makes it possible for CHECKMATE to happen.

In business, whether it be by voicemail, faxmail, email, snail mail or in person, CHECK is the moment of 'customer contact'. CHECK is that state of the customer's brain when it becomes possible for them to say YES or NO as a result of a contact from you. In other words, the customer's brain has been stimulated by a contact from you (CHECK) and so they will respond by deciding whether to act or not to act – YES or NO.

CHECK is when you ask the customer a question. It's when you mail the proposal, or when you send the email. It's when you show the video and lay out the details. It's when you fax out the press releases, and follow up with a telephone call. In show business, CHECK is performing the audition or sending out demo tapes of your songs. Sports people are in CHECK when they enter the competition.

CHECK is the activity you can use to manage the attention of the customer. In the customer's brain, attention is where the action is. The special strategic feature of the CHECK situation is: only the salesperson can control CHECK.

C

CHECK is the quintessence of business. In newsell, CHECK is the new metric, the fundamental unit of measurement. CHECK is the currency of your business and has its own symbol which is C.

UNCHECK

The Left position or OFF position of the newsell switch is UNCHECK. UNCHECK is whenever it is not possible for the customer to say NO or YES. UNCHECK is whenever you are not in contact with a customer or prospective customer (like now while you are reading this book). UNCHECK is the state of the customer's brain when it's not possible for them to say YES or NO. UNCHECK is the state of the customer's brain when it is just not attending to your offer.

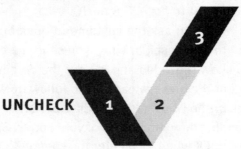

UNCHECK

Therefore, in business, UNCHECK is any moment when the customer cannot say either YES or NO because he or she is not, at that moment, in CHECK from a salesperson.

UNCHECK is all other business situations. You are in UNCHECK when you are carrying out all the routine chores of business that are necessary to keep you in business. You are in UNCHECK when you are buying a computer or seeing your accountant or arranging finance. UNCHECK is painting the office, record-keeping, writing reports and attending sales meetings. Doing research, buying stock, driving around the territory, listening to motivational CDs, designing a BVS, hiring and training – all of these are UNCHECK.

For writers, UNCHECK is doing research and writing the book. In show business it's learning lines, rehearsals and waiting tables. In sports, UNCHECK is training, travelling and coaching. Most of the time, we are in UNCHECK. UNCHECK is the groundwork, the preparation, the foundation of your business or career.

The paradox of UNCHECK is this:

While you cannot build a business without UNCHECK,
you cannot build a business with it!

UNCHECK Quicksand

The biggest oldsell trap is caused by sales managers undermining their salespeople by asking them 'Did you close the sale?' This question forces the salesperson to focus their field power on CHECKMATE – and this is the one area they *cannot* control. Eventually disappointment and rejection forces the individual back into the UNCHECK position.

Once a salesperson gets stuck in the quicksand of UNCHECK it inevitably leads to the demise of the salesperson. The business of business is to escape from UNCHECK and using the newsell switch – UNCHECKTOCHECK – is how we do it.

Switching from UNCHECKTOCHECK

The most strategic move in business is contacting a customer or escaping from UNCHECK to CHECK. In newsell, to help control this move, we use the brain software switch – pronounced 'Uncheck to Check' and written as UNCHECKTOCHECK.

● the move from UNCHECK to CHECK –
  UNCHECKTOCHECK

- the move from not being in contact with a customer to being in contact with a customer – UNCHECKTOCHECK
- the move from UNCHECK (when a customer cannot say either YES or NO) to CHECK (when a customer can say YES or NO) – UNCHECKTOCHECK
- attracting the attention of the customer's brain from not attending to your offer TO attending to your offer – UNCHECKTOCHECK
- switching from UNCHECK to CHECK more often than your competitor does is what succeeding in business is all about – UNCHECKTOCHECK
- your salespeople switching from UNCHECK to CHECK ten times more often than your competitor does is what newsell management is all about – UNCHECKTOCHECK X10.

UNCHECKTOCHECK

The only situation that can build your business is UNCHECKTOCHECK.

The only state that can accelerate your career is UNCHECKTOCHECK.

The only position that can create your fortune is UNCHECKTOCHECK.

The only move that can turn a customer into a client is UNCHECKTOCHECK.

According to the Newsell Theory of Selling:

To Check? or not to Check? *That* is the question.

11

UNCHECKTOCHECK

This is the most strategic move in business

'While the amateurs are discussing tactics,
the professionals are discussing logistics.'
– Military strategist

What is strategy? Take a moment here to write in the space the one word that you feel most describes the essence of strategy: _____.

If you ask this question of business leaders you get a wide variety of responses. I once had written responses from over 250 business leaders to this question and most chose words like 'planning' or 'action' (one CEO even said 'love'). My own view is that the single most important factor that describes strategy is 'control'.

If you cannot control it then it is not strategic for you. Carl von Clausewitz, whose book, *On War*, is one of the leading textbooks for military academies around the world, writes, 'Strategy fixes the point and the time where the battle is to be fought'. Control. The issue of strategy is the issue of control.

Because UNCHECKTOCHECK is the only situation 100 per cent controlled by you, UNCHECKTOCHECK is the most important strategic move in your business, your career or any other enterprise you wish to excel in. This control is the only feature that can guarantee you success; everything else is up for grabs.

Control

The three unique features of UNCHECKTOCHECK are:

1. UNCHECKTOCHECK is predictable
2. UNCHECKTOCHECK is controlled by you
3. UNCHECKTOCHECK means the next move is theirs.

Because UNCHECKTOCHECK is a strategic act or move, it is predictable. This predictability is a handle on the UNCHECKTOCHECK move that you can take hold of and use to your advantage. This predictability means you can devise a plan to use UNCHECKTOCHECK and then move to carry out your plan. You can manage UNCHECKTOCHECK.

Here are ten UNCHECKTOCHECK moves you can use:

1. You can send an email – UNCHECKTOCHECK
2. You can snailmail an invitation – UNCHECKTOCHECK
3. You can telephone with information – UNCHECKTOCHECK
4. You can fax a press release – UNCHECKTOCHECK
5. You can hold a conference, meeting or seminar – UNCHECKTOCHECK
6. You can perform an act of service – UNCHECKTOCHECK
7. You can put an ad on a web site – UNCHECKTOCHECK
8. You can ask a question – UNCHECKTOCHECK
9. You can visit with a gift – UNCHECKTOCHECK
10. You can have someone else do any of these on your behalf – UNCHECKTOCHECK.

The key points here are that all of these moves are predictable – you can plan to use them, and then no-one can stop you from enacting your plan. Once you act, the next move belongs to the customer. This is the essence of strategy.

UNCHECKTOCHECK

Of course, no idea is of any value until it is used. The same applies to this idea about UNCHECKTOCHECK – it's of no value unless you can use it. Why not take a strategic moment to list any ten specific acts or moves that you do in your business or career that are UNCHECKTOCHECK moves.

Before you start, here are some points to look for:

- UNCHECKTOCHECK must be a specific move that you can predict or plan in advance like giving a gift, or asking question
- UNCHECKTOCHECK is a move that you can control
- UNCHECKTOCHECK is a move that puts the ball in the customer's court.

NOTE:
It's important to remember UNCHECKTOCHECK is a process; not a result. We are not concerned with the result of the move here, whether or not the move 'worked'. We will cover results later.

Media for UNCHECKTOCHECK moves are:

1. Voicemail – UNCHECKTOCHECK done over the telephone
2. Email – UNCHECKTOCHECK sent email through cyberspace
3. Postmail – UNCHECKTOCHECK sent through the post
4. 'Meetmail' – UNCHECKTOCHECK where you meet the customer in person.

There are thousands of possible UNCHECKTOCHECK moves. I recently conducted a newsell seminar for a group of professional insurance agents and here are some of the UNCHECKTOCHECK moves they are using:

VOICEMAIL

UNCHECKTOCHECK – say hello and see how they are

UNCHECKTOCHECK – clarify a matter of possible confusion

UNCHECKTOCHECK – discuss a potential new opportunity

UNCHECKTOCHECK – get more information regarding customer's current needs

UNCHECKTOCHECK – review existing policies

UNCHECKTOCHECK – give the customer some information

UNCHECKTOCHECK – give the customer some recent information about you/your agency, eg new address

UNCHECKTOCHECK – perform an act of service

UNCHECKTOCHECK – thank the customer

UNCHECKTOCHECK – ask for a referral

UNCHECKTOCHECK – provide a teaser or tantaliser

UNCHECKTOCHECK – advise how plan is going, update

UNCHECKTOCHECK – make an offer

UNCHECKTOCHECK – extend an invitation

UNCHECKTOCHECK – tell the customer that you would like to visit him or her

UNCHECKTOCHECK – keep the relationship alive for future sales

UNCHECKTOCHECK – speak to a customer who cannot see you in person

EMAIL/POSTMAIL

UNCHECKTOCHECK – as a follow up on a live sales presentation

UNCHECKTOCHECK – send customer a proposal

UNCHECKTOCHECK – put URGENT sticker on envelope

UNCHECKTOCHECK – confirm accuracy of details of previous discussion

UNCHECKTOCHECK – mail an application

UNCHECKTOCHECK – send a gift

UNCHECKTOCHECK – ask for referral/s

UNCHECKTOCHECK – provide company literature

UNCHECKTOCHECK – tell him/her you plan to phone him/her for an appointment

UNCHECKTOCHECK – confirm details of an appointment

UNCHECKTOCHECK – make a recommendation
UNCHECKTOCHECK – present an idea
UNCHECKTOCHECK – introduce yourself/someone else
UNCHECKTOCHECK – offer congratulations/greetings
UNCHECKTOCHECK – send a bonus previously
promised
UNCHECKTOCHECK – send a thank you card/letter

MEETMAIL (IN PERSON)
UNCHECKTOCHECK – make a presentation
UNCHECKTOCHECK – conduct a demonstration
UNCHECKTOCHECK – perform an act of service
UNCHECKTOCHECK – provide information
UNCHECKTOCHECK – make the customer feel at
ease
UNCHECKTOCHECK – keep in touch
UNCHECKTOCHECK – introduce yourself
UNCHECKTOCHECK – get to know your customer
better
UNCHECKTOCHECK – take to your customer to lunch
UNCHECKTOCHECK – listen to what your customer has
to say
UNCHECKTOCHECK – ask for a referral
UNCHECKTOCHECK – pay your customer a compliment
UNCHECKTOCHECK – show your customer a new
opportunity
UNCHECKTOCHECK – test the progress of your
discussions and establish a
completion date

If you want you can select some of these examples or others and start to build your own list. Ten moves you can list on your UNCHECKTOCHECK list are:

1 I can _____

2 I can _____

3 I can _____

4 I can _____

5 I can _____

6 I can _____

7 I can _____

8 I can _____

9 I can _____

10 I can _____

There are, of course, hundreds of other UNCHECKTOCHECK moves for you to consider.

12

TTs – the Newsell Management System

The simple key performance indicator of the newsell strategy is the management and measurement of the daily TTs

It has become a cliché to say that 'Information is the principal commodity of our age' but it cannot be said enough that a clever company is one that gets a much better return on information. To do so, it needs not just one but two enterprise software upgrades. The two upgrades required are:

1. a business systems software upgrade and
2. a brain software upgrade.

In business, as in the military, we want to have an 'unfair' advantage over our competitors. Better flexibility in changing markets. Better customer response. Faster company growth. The clever company's success depends on the quality of its information and the speed with which that information can be shared throughout the enterprise. Recently, a client of mine made a $16 million investment in the SAP system – an enterprise-wide business software upgrade. SAP is one of the largest software companies in the world and has developed clever systems that enable companies of all sizes to link their business processes, tying together disparate business functions, and helping the whole enterprise run more smoothly.

My client's investment in SAP will integrate the entire organisation so information can be shared in real-time by employees, suppliers and distributors for a better return on information.

But, for a clever company to secure an unfair advantage over its competitors it can't do just what they do, it needs to do much more. For a MUCH better return on information the clever company must also take the opportunity to also invest in an upgrade of the brain software of the enterprise.

Augmenting the SAP investment, my client has also decided to upgrade the brain software currently being used by their employees, enterprise-wide.

Software for your brain

Your company's brains are currently using logic as your primary brain software. Logic was installed into stakeholders' brains by the education system which imported it from Europe 200 years ago. Logic was introduced into the European education system by Thomas Aquinas in the middle ages. Thomas got it from Plato and Aristotle. Logic was designed by these esteemed yet ancient Greeks 2500 years ago. There seems little point in expecting too much from a business software upgrade if the company's brains are still using 2500-year-old brain software!

Desktops and Necktops

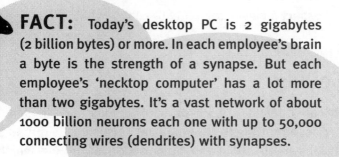

FACT: Today's desktop PC is 2 gigabytes (2 billion bytes) or more. In each employee's brain a byte is the strength of a synapse. But each employee's 'necktop computer' has a lot more than two gigabytes. It's a vast network of about 1000 billion neurons each one with up to 50,000 connecting wires (dendrites) with synapses.

So, multiply 1000 billion neurons by 50,000 synapses by the number of your company's employees ... Wow! That's a lot of enterprise brainpower leased monthly via the company payroll. The brainpower available to each employee's necktop is about 10,000 trillion bytes. To match that on a neuron-by-neuron basis a desktop would need to be able to perform 1 million, trillion arithmetic operations per second.

FACT: Compare any necktop with the largest supercomputers likely to be developed over the next decade. These will probably not attain speeds in excess of 1 trillion arithmetic operations per second which is about one-millionth of the computation rate of each of the necktops on the payroll.

FACT: The enterprise is preposterously over endowed with thinking hardware but it may be dangerously short on brain software. I would expect a clever company to change that.

Selling

To call oneself a 'salesperson' is just like, in some circles, admitting to cannibalism! This is partly due to a curious myth about the human skill of selling which should have been shattered long ago. The myth goes something like this: 'She is a good saleswoman because she has the gift of the gab', or 'He's a good talker. He should be a salesman.' This is just so much nonsense!

SELLING IS NOT A SKILL OF THE MOUTH,
SELLING IS A SKILL OF THE BRAIN!

If every week, on payday, your sales manager had to pin your paycheque on that part of your anatomy which is the source of your productivity – he would pin your paycheque on your head, because inside your head lies your ultimate profit centre.

What is the relationship between thinking and selling?

Thinking is the most fundamental and important human skill. Thinking is how we make use of information in order to control our behaviour. According to ancient wisdom, you are what you think – 'As a man thinketh in his heart, so is he'.

Skill in communication and the use and arrangement of information are what 'selling' or 'salesmanship' is all about. So is leadership. If you wish to change your behaviour, you first have to change what you think. If you wish to change someone else's behaviour, you are first going to have to help that person to change what he or she thinks.

Thinking is the ability to lead one's self. Leadership is the ability to get others to lead themselves. So is selling. Like all skills, these can be learned and developed.

Today, information is the currency of existence, and the value of information lies in the way it is arranged. Selling has to do with thinking. Selling has to do with information. Selling has to do with the way information is arranged and rearranged to get attention and then produce a change in human perception. Selling is the most fundamental and important social skill. It is a skill that anyone can develop provided he or she is willing to make the commitment to practise arranging and rearranging information.

And now we come to a critical insight about selling. This is also one of the great misunderstandings about selling and leadership. The most successful do understand it, the others don't. You will never, never, never break through until you own this insight about human behaviour. It has to do with being able to lead horses to water but not being able to make them drink. The critical insight is:

Only the salesperson controls CHECK
Only the customer controls CHECKMATE.

Since CHECKMATE, the decision to buy, is an electro-chemical event that happens in the brain of another individual, it's no surprise that you cannot control CHECKMATE. That is why there is no such thing as salespeople 'closing the sale' – only the customer can close the sale.

However, you can control the CHECK move which makes it possible (but not certain) that the customer may CHECKMATE.

There can be CHECK without CHECKMATE
but there can be no CHECKMATE without CHECK.

Feedback

How do you get the feedback you need to keep yourself on track? What can you do when you fall in a hole or get caught in a sales slump? One of the simplest tactics is to use questions.

Here are ten questions that you can ask yourself to produce the feedback you need to stay in control of how you plot your business course. Each question produces its own effect. Use the one you need to produce the effect you want, at any particular moment.

1 Ask yourself ... Am I doing UNCHECK, CHECK or CHECKMATE?

2 Ask yourself ... Why am I doing all this UNCHECK?

3 Ask yourself ... Why am I trying to CHECKMATE?

4 Ask yourself ... Why am I trapped in UNCHECK? How can I escape?

5 Ask yourself ... Why am I choosing CHECKMATE?

6 Ask yourself... What UNCHECKTOCHECK move can I control right now?

7 Ask yourself ... Where is my CHECKLIST?

8 Ask yourself ... What ten UNCHECKTOCHECK moves can I control today?

9 Ask yourself ... What UNCHECKTOCHECK moves can I use in this meeting?

10 Ask yourself ... What new UNCHECKTOCHECK moves can I use today?

Rejection and Call Reluctance

Whenever you get stuck in selling or leadership it's because you haven't asked yourself these ten questions. These ten questions are an instant antidote to rejection, call reluctance, and the other terminal sales diseases that are brought on by trying to CHECKMATE.

To any salesperson who is still trying to use 'clever closing techniques' – it's time to stop! You are now doing business in the new millennium. Leave the oldsell ideas of the 1950s behind and catch up to reality or you may miss out on the greatest business opportunities of today's global marketplace.

TT – the Newsell Management System

TT is a simple and powerful way to manage your two strategic business resources: time and energy. TT is the Newsell Management System and is an easy but laser-like system for the daily management of your

UNCHECKTOCHECK moves. TT focuses on two important business opportunities – Tomorrow and Today:

1 Tomorrow: every day you record the number of times you will try to perform UNCHECKTOCHECK in the next 24 hours.

2 Today: every day you record the number of times you were able to perform UNCHECKTOCHECK during the previous 24 hours.

Tomorrow

In the Newsell Management System, it's vital every day to take a stab at predicting how many UNCHECKTOCHECK moves you will do the next day. It doesn't matter what actually ends up happening. All that is required is that you try to guess at the number of UNCHECKTOCHECK moves you will do tomorrow.

Today

In the Newsell Management System, it's also vital every day to record exactly the number of UNCHECKTOCHECK moves you made the previous day. This includes all voicemail, email/postmail and 'meetmail' UNCHECKTOCHECK moves.

One Step Each Day

Just keeping these two Tomorrow/Today measurements every day may not seem like much to you now but, as you will soon see, when you do use the TT – Tomorrow/Today method you will be amazed at the results. Progress begins a step at a time. There is no sudden leap to greatness. Your success lies in what you do day by day. You will be in good company if you follow this advice and just record your Tomorrow/Today activity, a day at a time:

'The most successful men in the end are those whose success is the result of steady accretion ... It is the one who carefully advances step by step, with his mind becoming wider and wider, and progressively better able to grasp any theme or situation, persevering in what he knows to be practical, and concentrating his thought upon it, who is bound to succeed in the greatest degree.'
Alexander Graham Bell

'Perfection is attained by slow degrees; she requires the hand of time.'
Voltaire

'Little by little does the trick.'
Aesop

'All difficult things have their origin in that which is easy, and great things in that which is small.'
Lao-Tzu

'A jug fills drop by drop.'
Gautama Buddha

'Do not despise the bottom rungs
in the ascent to greatness.'
Publius Syrius

'Adopt the pace of nature; her secret is patience.'
Ralph Waldo Emerson

'God is in the details.'
Albert Einstein

Don't DYSH!

How to sabotage your own sales team

'Did you get the sale?'
– Sales Manager to salesperson

If you are a salesperson in a company, the reason you have a sales manager is because there are some things that machines can't yet do! These things are critical to the survival and success of any business. And what does a business need? A business needs productive humans.

Your managers get paid because of how they can help you to be more productive. Your managers are paid to help you to think! To learn! To notice! To create! To solve! To plan! To explain! To improve! To get along! To contribute! To produce! To CHECK!

Out Of Thin Air

A good manager can help you learn how to pull CHECK moves out of thin air. The UNCHECKTOCHECK strategy can literally produce new business out of thin air. How? Since UNCHECKTOCHECK is the only move that can produce new business – you either do it or you don't. You either make the move or you don't. You either escape from UNCHECK or you don't. If you don't, nothing will happen. If you do, something will happen. That something could be new business. Yes, you can just pull a CHECK move out of thin air.

Example: Years ago in New York, I saw a TV interview with Oprah Winfrey when she was starting out in her career as an actress. She said she read the Pulitzer Prize-winning novel, *The Colour Purple*, by Alice Walker. Two hours after reading the book she wrote to the author (UNCHECKTOCHECK) saying, 'You don't know me, but I just read your book and am devastated. I am an actress and if you ever make it into a movie please let me know. I'll do anything, I'll even play the venetian blinds just to be in it!'

Oprah also included reviews and details of her career. Alice Walker wrote back and they linked up with Stephen

Spielberg who subsequently directed the movie and Oprah was on her way. If that's not out of thin air, what is?

You can surely think of a personal example where by using UNCHECKTOCHECK you created an opportunity out of thin air that never would have happened if you didn't escape from UNCHECK.

The One-Second Escape

If I were asked what I felt was the most difficult feat in selling I would say, 'To escape from UNCHECK'.

How long does it take to escape from UNCHECK? It takes about one second to escape from UNCHECK:

- Voicemail? It takes one second to pick up the phone.
- Email/postmail? It takes one second to press SEND on an email or to drop a postcard in a mail box.
- 'Meetmail'? It takes one second to say, 'Hello' to another person.

Yes, I know there's more time involved in all these activities but right now I'm just focusing on the moment of escape from UNCHECKTOCHECK and that moment only takes a second.

84,600 a Day

If it only takes a second to escape from UNCHECK then how many of these escape moments are there each day?

The answer is 84,600! While I'm not suggesting we can ever harvest all of these moments each and every day, it shows that we are well-endowed with UNCHECKTOCHECK opportunities.

Sometimes, in my training seminars and workshops, I refer to the untapped business potential – UNCHECK – as the 'dark matter of the business universe'. Why? Because, every day, 99.99 per cent of all possible UNCHECKTOCHECK moves remain hidden. Like the dark matter of the universe, the opportunities to switch from UNCHECKTOCHECK mostly go unnoticed.

Even if a salesperson performed UNCHECKTOCHECK at the level of *8.4 times every day* (which would be high for many business people) that still means that 99.99 per cent of all possible UNCHECKTOCHECK moments remain untouched for that day. Just think!

Childish closing techniques are tired, old news. Do you travel around in a horse and cart? No. Well, why use even more antiquated sales and business methods?

Your manager can:

1 help you build your repertoire of UNCHECKTOCHECK moves, help you become more focused, help you get more done and be more in control so you can make more customer contacts or more sales calls

2 manage and reward your activity as measured on your daily TT Reports and help manage you by using the Ten Feedback Questions in Chapter 12.

The CHECKMATE/UNCHECK Loop

Nothing is better documented in business than the fact that the majority of salespeople and their managers are mediocre at selling. In fact, last year, 80 per cent of the nation's gross sales were made by only 20 per cent of the sales people. Research has shown that most of these selling failures (and, in selling, mediocrity is failure) are caught up running round and round, trapped in the CHECKMATE/UNCHECK loop. It goes something like this:

a   The sales person focuses his/her effort on CHECKMATE

b   Since s/he cannot control CHECKMATE s/he feels rejection, so

c   S/he switches off to UNCHECK and fills his or her time with 'busy' work

d   Salesperson stops doing the CHECK move and this is called 'call reluctance'.

DYSH?

By the way, would you like to know what is the most effective way to mismanage and sabotage a sales team? It's by DYSHing them. DYSH your salespeople and you are dooming them to UNCHECK via CHECKMATE. This can happen whenever they report in after a sales meeting by asking them the following question: Did You Sell Him? or Did You Sell Her? or D-Y-S-H? (Or any variation of DYSH such as Did you get the sale? Did they buy? Did you get the order? Did you close him? and so on.)

Your manager should *never* DYSH you. This is old-fashioned 'results-driven' management and has failed us miserably. DYSH tells you that management expects you to focus on CHECKMATE, which is impossible. When a salesperson is asked by their manager, 'Did you get the sale?' it switches that person straight into the CHECKMATE/UNCHECK loop and dooms them to the dreaded sales diseases of rejection, call reluctance, and ultimate failure. If you don't believe this. Test it. The facts are well documented.

UNCHECKTOCHECK

The newsell manager moves ahead with 'process-driven' management. The newsell manager asks: Did you CHECK a customer? Did you switch from UNCHECKTOCHECK? How many times did you escape from UNCHECK today? Can I have your TT Report? How can I help you increase your C moves?

The newsell manager uses more constructive questions like, 'Did you CHECK him, again?' 'What was his reaction?' 'What did you do then?' 'What is your next CHECK move' or any of the TEN FEEDBACK QUESTIONS, or your own variations on them. You manager can do nothing to manage CHECKMATE but s/he can bring a wealth of experience and corporate resources to the CHECK move.

KEY POINT: Your manager cannot manage results your manager can only manage the process that gets you results. Or, you cannot manage CHECKMATE you can only manage UNCHECKTOCHECK.

Sales managers! Please, don't DYSH your salespeople!

14

No Limits

Why there are no limits to newsell

'Your range of available choices –
right now – is limitless'
– Carl Frederick

'There is a great treasure there behind our skull ...
we have only learned a very, very small part of
what it can do.'
– Isaac Bashevis Singer

Limitations. What are they? Do they exist? Where do they come from? Are they real? Very often, limitations are in the eye of the beholder. One person sees a bottle of champagne as half empty, yet another sees it as half full; both are 'right'.

In general terms, limitations are the business of the Left Brain which packages up little patterns of our past experience for our future use. This, of course, is a very useful function of the Left Brain and saves us the bother of having to re-invent breakfast every morning.

Backing Into The Future

The downside of this is that we often find ourselves backing into the future, dragging our precious experience with us. We look at new information in terms of our experience: does it match? No, therefore it's 'wrong', and we discard it.

The future is the business of the Right Brain, which has no limitations. Unfortunately, our Western education which has made a god out of logic, has largely ignored the development of our Right Brain. We live in an age where our technology is in the 21st century but much of our thinking is still in the 15th century.

Right Brain Illiteracy

We know what a person looks like who is Left Brain-illiterate. Unable to read or write, it may be difficult for them to grasp opportunities and see concepts that require articulation. Yet many highly-educated and articulate people are Right Brain-illiterate. They are so full of their past experience, that they cannot escape from their point-of-view, and they cannot see the unlimited number of possible futures that are coming towards them. All they can see are the limitations of a set past which they try to impose on the future. There is, of course, no guarantee that the next decade will be the same as the last decade.

In business, if you are doing this year exactly what you did last year you are in deep fertiliser. You're being rapidly left behind.

History Shows

Western history is full of examples of this phenomenon. Left Brains trying to impose their limited experience on the unlimited possibilities of the Right Brain.

Here are some examples:

'Animals, which move, have limbs and muscles;
the earth has no limbs and muscles,
hence it does not move.'
– Scipio Chiaramonti, Professor of Mathematics,
Pisa, 1633 AD

'Woman may be said to be an inferior man.'
– Aristotle, Greek philosopher, 4th century BC

'Stocks have reached what looks like a permanently
high plateau.'
– Irving Fisher, Professor of Economics, Yale University,
17 October 1929

'I tell you Wellington is a bad general, the English are bad soldiers; we will settle the matter by lunchtime.'
– Napoleon, the morning of Waterloo

'*Jonathon Livingston Seagull* will *never* make it as a paperback.'
– James Galton, Publisher, 1972

'You'd better learn secretarial work or else get married.'
– Emmeline Snively, Director of Model Agency counseling Marilyn Monroe, 1944

'The horse is here to stay, but the automobile is only a novelty – a fad.'
– Bank President advising Horace Rackham (Henry Ford's lawyer) not to invest in Ford Motor Company, 1903

'The odds are now that the United States will not be able to honour the 1970 manned-lunar-landing date set by Mr Kennedy.'
– *New Scientist*, 30 April 1964

The netizens are coming!

It may be that limitations are an illusion caused by the inability of a person to balance their past experience stored in their Left Brain, with the unlimited possible futures which can be brought to them by their Right Brain.

Take the Internet, for example. As far as UNCHECKTOCHECK is concerned, there is no limit to its use. The Internet continues to grow at a great rate. Soon the net will have a billion hosts (individual computers with registered IP addresses). At the time of writing there are around 400 million hosts or 'netizens'; what does this mean? It means, look over the cyber-horizon, what can you see? They're coming! Six-hundred million of them – future netizens, future e-commerce customers.

The Net market is exploding and we can expect some extraordinary changes in every part of our system as the netizens keep coming in droves.

Millions of Millionaires

As time goes on it is becoming more and more difficult to avoid becoming a millionaire. For example, in the US in 1975, there were only 350,000 millionaire households or 0.5 percent of the population. By 2005, 5,600,000 households are estimated to be worth $1 million or more – 5.2 per cent of all US households – according to figures from the Affluent Market Institute. Baby boomers (and their children who stand to inherit $20 trillion over the next 20 years), represent the fastest growing segment of millionaires. Households in the $5 million category number about 328,000; while 38,000 have at least $10 million.

The same goes for Australia. In 1986 Australia had 25,000 millionaires. Recently Australia joined Singapore,

Hong Kong and India as being home to the world's largest growth in the number of millionaires. Australia has experienced nearly a 15 per cent increase in the number of high net-worth individuals, ranking ahead of the US, UK and Canada. Reporting on a study of global wealth distribution, Professor Yew Kwang Ng of Monash University, Economics Department, Melbourne says, 'Taking natural resources and leisure time into account, Australia is the wealthiest country in the world followed by Canada.'

This means that there are newsell opportunities on a scale never before experienced in history. There is no limit to the use of UNCHECKTOCHECK and the trend continues to be positive.

Tenpower

Simply add a zero

In coping with an environment of rapid change and the pressure of limitless opportunities, it's vital to have a strategic tool. In *Software for Your Brain* I examined putting the concept of *Tenpower* to work for you. Tenpower is a strategic measurement concept of the Right Brain which, when used skillfully, is hyper-productive in its results.

Tenpower is the habit of Powers of Ten. One way to use tenpower is to habitually multiply by ten (X10) or add a zero to whatever it is you are doing. So you can tenpower any CHECK move you are planning to make.

Newsell and Tenpower:

UNCHECKTOCHECK X10

For example, if you are:

- planning to C with a press release ... send out 10 press releases – tenpower
- sending out ten demo tapes ... send out a 100 demo tapes – tenpower
- looking for a gift for someone ... look for 10 gifts for someone – tenpower
- putting ten people on your email list? ... put 100 on your list – tenpower.

No-one can stop you from doing this but yourself. You may not have the resources to use tenpower all the time but you can use it more often than now ... ten times more often.

Do you get the idea? It takes a little getting used to (so do the results!) but if you practise using tenpower, say, TEN TIMES, it will become a habit. No doubt you can imagine the unfair strategic advantage that moving through information by powers of ten gives the user over someone who is just incrementing along at the rate of 10 per cent at a time, the standard, traditional business rate. So, accelerate into your future with tenpower and watch what happens. With tenpower you now have everything you need to become a soaring success with UNCHECKTOCHECK.

List ten ways you can use tenpower in your business or life over the next ten days:

1. I can use tenpower to increase _____

_____

2. I can use tenpower to increase _____

_____

3. I can use tenpower to start _____

_____

4. I can use tenpower to start _____

_____

5. I can use tenpower to do _____

_____

6. I can use tenpower to do _____

_____

7. I can use tenpower to practise _____

_____

8. I can use tenpower to practise _____

_____

9. I can use tenpower to try _____

_____

10. I can use tenpower to give _____

_____

Now you can add tenpower to your C moves since this is part of the strategy of newsell.

UNCHECKTOCHECK X10 ... do it well, TEN TIMES better.

UNCHECKTOCHECK X10 ... do it often, TEN TIMES more often.

Here are ten UNCHECKTOCHECK switches sent in by trainees. There's nothing sacred about these ten, they are just ten UNCHECKTOCHECK moves chosen at random. We could just as easily choose a different ten. Some work better by voicemail, others as postmail or email, and others as 'meetmail' but most of them can be used in all three types of UNCHECKTOCHECK situations.

Questions

By the way, questions are the ideal UNCHECKTOCHECK moves. When you are interacting with a prospect or customer or another person, UNCHECKTOCHECK is very effective with questions. You ask a question then you listen to the answer and then you can ask the next question. While you cannot control the answers you can always control the questions and that's enough to make 'the question' a classic UNCHECKTOCHECK move.

What follows is a random selection of ten UNCHECKTOCHECK moves:

UNCHECKTOCHECK – I couriered ... the artwork
UNCHECKTOCHECK – I phoned ... a desirable
candidate for a position with us
and I invited him/her to apply for
the position
UNCHECKTOCHECK – I gave ... samples of our new
product to our customers to use
in their business as a test
UNCHECKTOCHECK – I invited ... prospects to an all-
expenses one-day plant tour of
our company
UNCHECKTOCHECK – I started ... a new 90-day
intensive training program (using
outside consultants) for associate
realtors before an associate can
be placed in a branch office
UNCHECKTOCHECK – I gave ... as an offer, a free
portfolio appraisal to demonstrate
how I can improve clients' current
income with a repositioning of
their assets in their portfolio
UNCHECKTOCHECK – I SMSed ... a client how he could
improve his/her company's cash
flow by 20 per cent, thereby
improving his bottom line
UNCHECKTOCHECK – I mailed ... 85 invitations to my
in-laws' 50th anniversary and
enclosed a stamped return
envelope for the RSVP

UNCHECKTOCHECK – I phoned ... the president of a company and suggested he consider negotiating a contract (for a building) instead of bidding the contract out for tender

UNCHECKTOCHECK – I showed ... prospects a new and different way they can evaluate quality when assessing the type of products I sell (furs).

IMPORTANT NOTE: The emphasis here is on the *process* not the *result*. We are interested in designing UNCHECKTOCHECK moves and building a repertoire of customer-contact moves and carrying them out. We are not hung-up on the result. We are not obsessed with 'closing the sale'. Just carry out the move, notice what happens and start again.

Profit
AND
The WOMBAT Strategy

3

Profit

Profit is not a dirty word

> **profit** n: 1 an advantage or benefit.
> 2 financial gain. 3 excess of returns over outlay.
> – Oxford English Dictionary

This part of the book has been written for those who want to go beyond the theory of newsell and put it into practice. It will show you simply and effectively how you can use newsell to build your own profits in just 100 days.

I recently read in the news an interview with the retiring CEO of one of Australia's biggest companies. He was an American who had been recruited to lead this large business and had done a great job. Now he was retiring back to the States. He had enjoyed his stay here and he found Australians to be friendly and hospitable, but he made an interesting observation: he noticed in

Australia that the word 'profit' was often a bad word. It was a word that seemed to smell, in some circles, even frowned upon, in others. He thought this was because the word and the concept were widely misunderstood. On reflection, I agreed with him.

Whether we like it or not, we live in a world that is powered by profit. People talk about 'making a profit'. Companies succeed and make profits or fail and make losses. Are profits bad? Should we make profits? What happens if we don't make a profit? Who cares?

What is profit?

Let's start with a dictionary definition more complete than the one above.

> **profit** n: 1 an advantage or benefit. 2 financial gain; excess of returns over outlay. v: 1 be beneficial to 2 obtain an advantage or benefit (profited by the experience). profit and loss account: an account in which gains are credited and losses debited so as to show the net profit or loss at any given time. profit margin: the profit remaining in a business after costs have been deducted. profit-sharing: the sharing of profits especially between employer and employees. profit-taking: the sale of shares etc at a time when profit will accrue. (Latin profectus progress).
> – Oxford English Dictionary

We need the concept of profit in a healthy human society. If we look beyond immediate selfish needs, then we will have to invest in the future, to plan ahead, to take risks. None of these things would be attractive without the concept of profit.

Profit means gain, financial or otherwise, and the potential for gain enables us to look to the future.

Profit = Gain

We can profit or gain by:

- going to school and building our knowledge-base
- learning new skills to gain an advantage in sport
- travelling around our country or to other countries to profit by more experiences
- going online by investing in a computer, the Internet and software to gain an advantage in productivity
- starting a business by providing a service to people who will gain an advantage.

This last example is what I do in my consulting practice.

Profits = Jobs

Australia has one of the highest teenage suicide rates in the world. Despair is one of the contributing factors and one of the things some young people despair of is their inability to find a job. Unemployment is a problem not only for Australia but for many countries and it needs to be reduced. Growth is needed to reduce unemployment. The more growth in the economy the more jobs are created.

Profit = Investment

What is the role of profits in sustaining growth? Profits are needed for investment capital and investment is fundamental for growth.

In his seminal work, *Scale and Scope of Industrial Capitalism*, Alfred Chandler of Harvard Business School examined the histories of 200 of the largest and most successful manufacturing companies in the US, Britain and Germany over the past century.

FACT: A key ingredient in their success was that they all made large investments in the following areas.

1   Production facilities. The investments were large enough to take advantage of economies of scale and scope.

2   People. They made strategic investments in recruiting and organising employees and managers capable of running the enterprise efficiently.

Today, these successful companies continue their investment strategy by investing in software, communications and networking facilities to enhance their growth.

The detailed research of economic historians, such as Chandler, highlights the importance of profits for long-term success of individual companies. A high level of profits encourages investment, not just in machines, but in the company's workforce, in R&D, in new methods of working, in distribution and in marketing networks.

Investment = Growth

Economic growth depends in part on investment. Capital investment encompasses not only hard assets like plant and equipment but also people – intellectual capital.

The more that companies invest in the skills of their workforce the more other companies have to do so to keep up. This sets off a growth cycle. These investment benefits are not only internal for the good of the company but also external for the good of the economy.

Profit = Investment = Growth

Investments are usually a fixed proportion of profits. The higher the profits the higher the investments. Profit = investment.

Since the rate of investment determines the rate of growth of the economy, the higher the investment the greater the growth. Investment = growth.

The underlying growth rate of the economy is determined by the rate of investment, which in turn depends upon the share of profits in national income. Profit = investment = growth.

Economic policies to promote growth should therefore aim:

1　either to encourage a higher rate of investment for any given level of profitability or

2　to increase profits.

This is why the goals of clever companies have always been long-term profit and long-term growth. These goals were first established in America and subsequently in Japan and Germany. They are still the goals of the world's most successful companies today and goals which the rising economies of the far east are successfully exploiting.

Profit and Clever Government

Clever governments need policies which make for clever people and clever companies. The productivity of clever people and the profitability of clever companies should be more prominent in public policy than it is at present because raising productivity and raising profits is one way to achieve a higher rate of growth in the long term.

In the short term, however, higher profits do mean that less income is available to other sectors of the economy, in particular to wage and salary earners whose share of national income is by far the largest of any individual sector. Intelligently balancing the immediate demands of wages against the long-term demands of investment is what makes a clever government.

Profit Means Gain

Profit encourages investment in the future by producing a gain or advantage of some kind. List three examples each of how you profited or gained from various investments you have made, both financial and intellectual:

GAINS FROM FINANCIAL INVESTMENTS

1 _____

2 _____

3 _____

GAINS FROM INTELLECTUAL INVESTMENTS

1 _____

2 _____

3 _____

PROFIT MEANS INVESTMENT

When you've made a profit from an investment you can either:

1 take the profit or
2 rollover some of that profit in a further investment.

List one example of each of the above from your own experience.

PROFIT-TAKING

1 _____

INVESTMENT

2 _____

The Big Three

Who are the greatest marketing geniuses?

As I write, it is August 28, the feast day of Saint Augustine who, in my opinion, was the greatest marketing genius in history. My other two nominations are George Gallup and Tim Berners-Lee. Here's the thinking behind my three choices: Saint Augustine invented the first loyalty program which helped grow the most successful human organisation in history; George Gallup invented market research and delivered ultimate power to the customer; Tim Berners-Lee invented the World Wide Web and the opportunity for global e-commerce, 24/7.

Augustine of Hippo (354–430 CE)

On the Vatican website, I found the following announcement:

> ### DECREE OF THE APOSTOLIC PENITENTIARY
> ### ON SPECIAL INDULGENCES CONCEDED
> ### FOR THE 20TH WORLD YOUTH DAY IN COLOGNE
>
> **A Plenary Indulgence is conceded on the usual conditions (sacramental Confession, Eucharistic Communion and prayers for the Supreme Pontiff's intentions) to members of the faithful who, in a spirit of total detachment from any sin, will take part attentively and devoutly in some of the celebrations for the *20th World Youth Day* in Cologne.**

Just in case, like myself, you're not a member of the faithful, the announcement above means that those members who qualify are *guaranteed* to get into heaven when they die. This is a very big offer for any member of the faithful. It's called a plenary indulgence.

A plenary indulgence is a guarantee that you will receive enough frequent flyer points – divine grace – to go directly to heaven when you die. Like any other loyalty program there are rules and conditions and the Vatican lays these out from time to time. In this particular case, to qualify for a plenary indulgence a member must have gone to confession, taken communion, prayed for the Pope and attended the 20th World Youth Day in Cologne. Those members who observed these conditions are guaranteed by the Vatican to receive a sufficient allotment of grace to be admitted into Civitas Dei, the City of God – aka heaven.

The popularity of books like *The Da Vinci Code* reveals the fascination that the Vatican holds for many people – members and non-members alike – and I have always thought that the offer of VIP passes into Heaven is one of the cleverest ever invented. The evidence of history has shown how well it has worked. It continues to do so today. This particular invention was created by Saint Augustine.

For any loyalty system to be successful you need several things:

- **Currency. Some kind of points system.**
- **Rewards and punishments. Rules for getting points and for losing them.**
- **Destination. A desirable destination that motivates members to play.**

Saint Augustine invented the idea of 'original sin' which meant that all members of the faithful arrived into the world with debit points – just for being born!

Prior to Augustine a newborn baby might be expected to go straight to heaven. After Augustine, babies already had debit points in their heaven account. These debit points had to be wiped out first and then further points were needed to get into heaven. This meant that playing the loyalty game was no longer an option to members. After Augustine you *had* to play the game because your account was already in the red.

How do you remit your sins and collect the heaven points, the grace needed to get into heaven? This is where the Vatican comes in. The Curia devised a scheme where points were awarded for a wide range of Vatican-approved activities. For example, members have been able to earn points by praying at certain times in certain formats, by attending Vatican-approved sacraments and events. By doing certain good works. By making donations, or raising an army for the Pope or leaving property to the church when you die.

In 1343, Pope Clement VI confirmed that the Catholic Church can grant remission of sin through indulgences:

Upon the altar of the Cross Christ shed of His blood not merely a drop, though this would have sufficed, by reason of the union with the Word, to redeem the whole human race, but a copious torrent ... thereby laying up an infinite treasure for mankind. This treasure He neither wrapped up in a napkin nor hid in a field, but entrusted to Blessed Peter, the key-bearer, and his successors, that they might, for just and reasonable causes, distribute it to the faithful in full or in partial remission of the temporal punishment due to sin.

Loyalty programs can backfire if they exploit their members. The best example of this was when Pope Leo X (born Giovanni di Lorenzo de' Medici) used the scheme to raise money for his lavish lifestyle and vast Vatican construction projects. Martin Luther blew the whistle on the Pope and the Vatican subsequently lost a big share of the market. This became known in history as the Reformation and led to the establishment of the Protestant churches who broke away from the Vatican because of its loyalty scheme. Commenting on the proceeds of the scheme Martin Luther wrote:

> 'At the time I did not yet know who was to get the money. Then there appeared a booklet with the illustrious coat of arms of the Bishop of Magdeburg.'
> **Wider Hans Worst, 1541**

The Vatican still uses the scheme which has been copied by many marketing organisations worldwide, especially in the travel industry. This is not surprising since Augustine's original invention relied on a member's belief in the premise that the Vatican was the official travel agent for the City of God.

For example, Virgin Blue airlines' loyalty program called Velocity was promoted with headlines such as, 'Isn't it time loyalty programs redeemed themselves?' The main benefit of Velocity over other loyalty programs is its ability to redeem your points sooner rather than later. This draws attention to the main drawback of the

Vatican's loyalty program: that you have to die before you can redeem your points.

George Gallup (1901–1984)

Professor George Gallup developed the concept of the statistical sample and invented market research and polling. He got into research when he was an editor of the *Daily Iowan* at the University of Iowa and later an interviewer for D'Arcy Advertising in 1922. He became interested in the way people read newspapers and in particular which stories they actually read.

Gallup adopted the startling device of confronting a reader with the whole newspaper and asking him exactly what he liked and did not like about it. This gave him the material for a PhD thesis, 'An objective method for determining the reader interest in newspapers.' His thesis was based on a survey of the editorial and advertisement content of *The Des Moines Register and Tribune* and he found out that most readers preferred comics to the front page, feature stories to news.

He then adapted his ideas to advertising. If an advertiser could ask a population their opinions of a product or an advertisement that would be of enormous help in evolving better offers and ads. The problem was that it would be too expensive and time consuming to ask an entire population for their viewpoints.

Gallup showed that by using a statistical sample of around 1200 people you could reflect an accurate opinion of the entire population (plus or minus a few points) and this could be done inexpensively and regularly. Prior to Gallup, marketers like Henry Ford got away with offers like, 'You can have it in any colour as long as it's black'. Today, no competent marketer of products, services or political candidates would go to the people without first using market research and/or polling science to find out what they think. The Gallup Poll at Princeton – http://www.gallup.com – still has the best record for predicting the outcome of Presidential elections in the US over the past 70 years.

Gallup's invention may be the single greatest act of empowerment given to customers and to electors that has ever been invented by any scientist.

Sir Tim Berners-Lee

In declaring Sir Tim Berners-Lees to be one of the most important people of the 20th century, *Time* magazine said:

'From the thousands of interconnected threads of the Internet, he wove the World Wide Web and created a mass medium for the 21st century'.

Unlike so many inventions that forever changed the world, the World Wide Web – WWW – was the work of just one man. Edison had a lab full of people working on the light bulb for which he got the credit. And this is normally the case. The Internet itself was made by committee with its protocols and packet switching. *Time* magazine says, 'The World Wide Web is Berners-Lee's alone. He designed it. He loosed it on the world. And he more than anyone else has fought to keep it open, nonproprietary and free'.

Berners-Lee's invention was based on an information retrieval program called Enquire which he wrote in 1980 as a contract programmer at the European Organization for Nuclear Research (CERN) in Geneva, Switzerland. The soft-spoken programmer founded the World Wide Web Consortium (http://www.w3.org) at MIT, which he still directs, to promote global Web standards.

The WWW has made e-commerce a reality. It's business heaven, 24/7. You can point-and-click anywhere on the planet. You can search the libraries of the world, even the Vatican archives. You can get music, videos and sex. You can buy books or sell junk. You can get education, ideas and online help. You can have your say without persecution. You can do your banking and pay your bills. You can publish a book and sell it online and get paid without a publisher. You can book a flight and a hotel room anywhere on the planet. You can receive healthcare, create wealth, enhance your productivity and monitor your security – all on the WWW – and without ever leaving your home. You could even do it all while lying on the beach.

Today there are over 70 million websites. I was able to put the School of Thinking (SOT) on the web in 1995 when it became one of the first 10,000 websites. SOT lessons are still being sent out daily to over 50 countries from www.schoolofthinking.org thanks to Berners-Lee's invention.

E-commerce has already changed media and advertising spending in the big corporate budgets. Huge chunks of traditional advertising and marketing dollars are now being spent online. In 2004, Chrysler decided to spend 10 per cent of their US$2 billion pool of ad dollars online. In 2005 it was 18 per cent and in 2006 it will be more than 20 per cent. If you do the maths that's over $400 million in 2006 that used to be spent on ads in the *Wall Street Journal*, *USA Today* or NBC TV that are now being spent on the WWW. In an interview with *Fortune* magazine in 2005 about e-commerce trends, Julie Roehm, Chrysler's Director of Marketing Communications explained her decision, 'I hate to sound like a marketing geek but we like to fish where the fish are'.

Thanks to e-commerce on the WWW, Google has been making big profits from selling online ads. These profits have driven its stock prices to make it the most highly prized media company in the world, capitalised at over US$85 billion.

There will be powerful competition in the coming years for the multibillion-dollar global online marketing and communications budgets. As the advertising slogan goes: watch this space!

WOMBAT Marketing

Why WOMBATs always win in the end

'WOMBAT stands for Word of Mouth Buy And Tell.
This is a very simple system which is easy to
replicate because most ten year olds are
already good at it.'
– *The X10 Memeplex*, Michael Hewitt-Gleeson

Everyone is a WOMBAT. All the time. This is the most
valuable insight in this book and the more you get this
insight, the more you'll get from this book. Here it is
again: Everyone is a WOMBAT. All the time!

Oldsell is 'close driven'. Oldsell is about sales managers DYSHing their salespeople with the mantra, 'Did you close the sale?' or 'Did you get the order?'. The strategy of newsell has been to look at selling from the customer's viewpoint, not the sales manager's. Newsell recognises that the customer closes the sale, not the salesperson.

In fact, as customers, we are *all* closing sales, all the time. We are buying ideas and opportunities, goods and services all day long. We are always telling others about our new ideas, our favourite products and the latest services. In fact, everyone is buying and telling all the time. Yes, we are all WOMBATs and we know a lot about how WOMBATs think, how they behave and what they like and dislike.

For example:

- WOMBATs like to be first.
- We like to share.
- Show off.
- Help out and be helped.
- We like to flirt with other WOMBATs.
- We like to influence them and, in turn, we like to win the approval of other WOMBATs.
- Sometimes we like to be Ambassadors.
- Other times, we like to be waited on and served.
- WOMBATs do like rewards but we are also wary and suspicious when they are offered too easily.
- Some WOMBATs are free and independent.
- They replicate for their own reasons, not for yours.

- WOMBATs do love recognition. We appreciate feedback.
- Especially when it is sincere, fair and objective.
- WOMBATs distrust salesmanship.
- Sometimes we are entertained by it but we don't necessarily buy it.
- WOMBATs trust WOMBATs.
- WOMBATs hate being boxed-in, corralled or pressured.
- We detest being manipulated and we warn other WOMBATs.
- WOMBATs can be fooled but we are not suckers.
- WOMBATs are reliable friends but we can be devoted enemies.
- WOMBATs are not bees – we don't buzz. We buy and tell.
- We are often unpredictable because we have our own secret networks and connections. Our contacts cross generations, neighbourhoods, communities and hemispheres.
- WOMBATs have friends in unexpected places.
- WOMBATs have a limited attention span. We get bored. We tire of things.
- We like to participate. We don't like being lectured.
- WOMBATs do love stories. We like to tell them and we like to hear stories from other WOMBATs.
- We love gossip. It's how we relate to one another. We love stories about sex, scandals, lies and 'closed doors'.

- WOMBATs like secrets and stories about the bizarre and unusual. Why? Because we love to get a good laugh from another WOMBAT so we pass on stories that are hilarious, outrageous and naughty.

These are the reasons why WOMBATs give other WOMBATs their undivided attention. And, as a WOMBAT, you already know this from your own experience.

'Take Home' Value

WOMBATs can be CEOs and presidents of corporations. Most of my consulting activities involve coaching or working with CEOs and their organisations. Often, I'm invited to speak to groups of WOMBAT CEOs.

The TEC groups (The Executive Connection) in Australia and New Zealand are membership groups of WOMBAT CEOs, while in the US, the YPO (Young Presidents Organisation) is an international body of chief executive officers of established companies who became members by the age of 40. They are all WOMBATs through local chapter meetings, regular regional conferences, and their international 'universities' where they share with each other a world-class structure for personal and professional development, financial support and business leads. They also enjoy a mutual support network for the unique problems faced by the chief executive of a modern corporation.

A few years ago, YPO headquarters in Texas asked me to speak to a conference of about 45 YPOers responsible for planning their regional conferences around the world for the coming year. Inevitably, the YPOers at the conference raised the question, 'What about 'take home' value?' 'Take home' value is a specific, useable idea, tip, ploy or tactic that delegates can take home from the conference and put to use immediately in their own businesses. Wisely, they don't want to waste their time with fuzzy, esoteric, nonsense of an impractical nature.

So, I said to the group (who were by now familiar with CVSTOBVS), 'If your current view of the situation (CVS) is "take home" value, let's now go beyond that and look for a better view of the situation (BVS)'. In the discussion that followed the BVS that they moved up to was 'pass on' value.

'Pass On' Value

'Pass on' value applies to an idea that is not just good enough for you to take home and use yourself but one that is so simple, elegant and robust that you can pass it on to your family, colleagues, employees, customers or friends. From 'take home' value to 'pass on' value, from CVSTOBVS.

Pass on value is all about replication. It's that quality of an information package that makes it very likely to be passed on by recipients and so to replicate itself again and again, many times over.

Example: Let's take a joke. You'll have heard some jokes; most of them in fact, that as soon as they're told you may laugh a little but that's it. You forget them. Then there is the joke that is so funny, so to the point, so timely that you just can't wait to tell someone = 'pass on' value.

The same applies to gossip. All good gossip has, by definition, pass on value. Most juicy gossip with great pass on value usually begins with the phrase, 'Promise you won't tell anyone but you'll die when you hear what happened to ...'

Replication

The quintessence of a BVS is pass on value. When I am designing a BVS I try to ensure that it has pass on value – an arrangement of information so powerful that it replicates itself. When one human brain so influences another human brain that it reaches the point of changing its CVS to a new BVS, this brain-to-brain messaging, in business, is called Word-of-Mouth advertising.

Oxford Professor Richard Dawkins, who has called this pass on effect 'replicator power', says that it is the genetic effect of certain information to replicate itself:

'As part of their equipment, bodies evolved on-board
computers – brains. Brains evolved the capacity to
communicate with other brains by means of language
which opens up new possibilities for self-replicating
entities. The new replicators are not DNA. They are
patterns of information that can thrive only in brains or
in the artificially manufactured products of brains –
books, computers and so on. But, given that brains,
books and computers exist, these new replicators,
which I call "memes" to distinguish them from genes,
can propagate themselves from brain to brain, from
brain to book, from book to brain, from brain to
computer, from computer to brain.'
The Blind Watchmaker

Memes

Dawkins' 'Meme' meme has itself caught on and is
widely discussed on the Internet. There are newsgroups
and others who are interested and a whole area called
'memetics' has sprung up. Much of the discussion seems
to misunderstand Dawkins' idea but it is fun to check it
out. If you are interested you can do a Yahoo search for
'memes' and 'memetics'. I have written in *The X10
Memeplex* about how memes acquire brain space in
people (WOMBATs) and get themselves spread around.

The School of Thinking also offers training in
memetic thinking as part of the newsell training
(www.schoolofthinking.org).

Selling as Replication

The time has come when we can look at a salesperson as the part s/he plays in the 'replication of the product meme'. The product meme is the special information package, the business BVS, entrusted to the salesperson by his or her company. The salesperson acts as the replicator, who passes a BVS on to A, who passes it on to B, who passes it on to C.

For some, this discussion on memes may seem tangential, others will see the opportunity this link gives for marketing to harvest some exciting scientific work that is going on in this field.

Word-of-Mouth or WOM

When this kind of approach to selling is properly understood and structured, it is the most efficient, profitable and powerful selling strategy that has yet been devised. Regis McKenna at www.mckenna-group.com who helped put the Macintosh computer on the map says, 'Word-of-mouth is probably the most powerful form of communication in the business world'.

It certainly worked on me. My Chicago lawyer friend Peter Bensinger Jr (once called the 'most wired lawyer in America') told me about the Mac when it first came out over 20 years ago. We both bought one. We got online and played a computer game about World War II submarine warfare called Gato. We did it for hours and hours on end.

Since then I've bought dozens of Macs and told thousands of people how great they are. I'm a WOMBAT.

No doubt you are familiar with this kind of scenario. A friend told you about a movie that she really liked and encouraged you to go see it. You saw the movie and liked it so much that you told another friend and he went to the movie and so on. That's because you're a WOMBAT too.

This, of course, isn't new. It's every marketing director's dream and word-of-mouth advertising is the oldest and still considered to be the most effective of all advertising strategies.

Three of the most common WOM (word-of-mouth) applications are:

1. COI – Centre of Influence
2. MLM – Multi-Level-Marketing and
3. Affiliate Marketing.

Centre of Influence

In any population sub-group, such as a target audience or a market niche, the 10 per cent lead the 90 per cent. There is usually a small group of heavy-hitters who call the shots and are known in the trade as a COI (centre of influence). COIs may be a handful of trade journalists, a few market-leaders, some early innovators, an industry spokesperson, a recognised guru or a high-profile customer. When these people talk the rest of the target audience listens.

Every marketing plan or personal sales plan should seriously consider who should be on the COI list. Who are the influential top ten VIPs that you have on your COI list?

WOM + Money = MLM

One of the most controversial marketing phenomena of the past 20 years is multi-level marketing (MLM). Starting out as pyramid-schemes, like Holiday Magic in the late 1960s, they soon attracted the attention of the legislators. Pyramid schemes are now illegal and most schemes have evolved into network or multi-level marketing, otherwise known as MLM.

The MLM twist to traditional WOM adds the reward of money. It can be a very interesting idea because it means that the customer also becomes the marketer and has the potential of harnessing the most powerful trick in the universe.

Long ago and far away (millions of light years) a molecule happened that was different to all other molecules that had ever existed. The unique difference was that this molecule could reproduce itself. It could replicate. And so, from this special molecule evolved DNA and genes and everything that has ever lived on the planet!

If genes couldn't replicate, then you wouldn't be reading this now because neither you nor I nor this paper would ever have existed. Genetic replication is a very clever trick and is the most powerful fact of life that we know.

The mathematics of replication produce staggering numbers. If we hop from genetics back to marketing we can see the potential of the idea of the customer also becoming the marketer. This would mean that customers could self-replicate. Five customers could soon become 25 then 125, 625, 3125, 15,625, 78,125, 390,625, 1,953,125, 9,765,625. That's around 10 million customers from 5 after just 10 generations. And indeed, this is what *can* happen, in theory, when customers self-replicate, creating new customers, who also self-replicate and so on.

One of the reasons that it doesn't happen, in reality, is because most people are reluctant to sell to their friends, and as soon as this occurs, the replication ceases. Anyone in MLM knows this from their own experience. The more successful MLMers are those who go beyond their friends.

In the last two decades, MLM became one of the fastest growing marketing models in the world but is now in decline. Unfortunately, due to oldsell, the potential has been spoiled. Some MLM programs have a quasi-religious spin on them which has caused a negative reaction amongst customers in the marketplace. For example, a few years back a notorious American soap MLM organisation was successfully sued by the large conventional soap company, Procter and Gamble. In their defence, these crusading MLMers claimed that Procter and Gamble was the work of 'the devil'.

Most people tell me they have been subjected to high pressure, misrepresentation, even lying to customers in what is called 'the curiosity approach' by these oldsell operations. This type of oldsell behaviour spoils the marketplace and only demonstrates how little these MLM practitioners really understand WOM and replication systems. Even the punitive court actions against them have done little to change their oldsell behaviour or to win back the customers' respect.

On the other hand, there are many quality direct-selling and MLM organisations who are widely respected by their distributors and customers alike. Some provide realistic business platforms for their distributors with no capital required. These companies offer a clever product mix with a sensible, long-term, marketing plan. These can also be maximised using newsell.

The Clever MLMer

For over 20 years I have been fascinated by MLM systems. There are two varieties: get-rich-quick and build-your-business. The vast majority of people have failed to meet their expectations. This is mostly due to the hyped-up, unrealistic oldsell expectations that are widely proclaimed by greedy get-rich-quick merchants. Caveat emptor. Yet I have known a small minority of people who have met and even surpassed all their expectations. By using the build-your-business attitude and servicing a retail network of satisfied customers these people receive healthy monthly incomes which steadily increase as each satisfied customer WOMs the product and evolves into a downline sub-distributor.

The most successful and clever MLMers have one Golden Rule:

Never accept a new distributor downline unless they are already a satisfied retail customer. No exceptions!

A satisfied customer is one who is WOM-qualified. Evidence of this is a customer who has bought and used the product at retail and then wants to re-order. Such a customer is genuinely qualified to WOM. Only then, at the earliest, does a clever MLMer allow such a customer to become a sub-distributor. Those who understand replication systems can use this policy to build a strong and deep MLM business in 12 to 36 months.

Devils and Wombats

In working with MLM organisations, I try to help them choose a newsell style. I point out they can choose between two contrasting strategies: devils and wombats.

The devil-style is oldsell and DEVIL stands for Daily Enthusiastic Victories and Inspirational Leadership. Few people have escaped contact with these Rah! Rah! Rah! sect-like schemes of the follow-the-leader variety. They are famous for their exaggerated claims, their intimidation and high-pressure, oldsell sales tricks.

Devils often begin their new customer relationship with a lie like, 'Come over to my place for a coffee'. When you get there it's a sales pitch for an MLM company. Some devil-style organisations encourage this and call it the 'curiosity approach'. I call it the stupidity approach. It's hard to see how you could abuse a customer more than to begin the relationship with a lie!

By contrast there is the wombat-style of MLM system. This is a newsell style and WOMBAT stands for Word-Of-Mouth Buy And Tell. This is a pure system which is simple to replicate because most ten-year-olds can do it. It sticks to the Golden Rule mentioned above and is built only on a rock-solid base of satisfied customers who:

1 first *buy* the product at retail. Then
2 when they are satisfied, they *tell* others about it.

This is the true WOMBAT: Word of mouth through buy and tell.

In my experience the wombats outlast the devils 100 to 1. I only wish I had been taught about it when I was ten years old. With compound interest I would have been a millionaire by the time I was called up for Viet Nam!

Affiliate Marketing

One facet of Internet marketing is called 'affiliate marketing'. Amazon.com is probably the best-known example but there is an ever-increasing number of affiliate marketing schemes. Many of these schemes are oldsell and are copies of the direct-mail schemes of the 1980s which have been exported to the online environment. These are characterised by using email to spam prospective customers on a large scale. Spam is electronic 'junk mail'.

Customer complaints have caused the legislators to crack down on spammers with many countries introducing privacy laws. Many other affiliate programs, like Amazon, use opt-in/opt-out or permission marketing to differentiate themselves from the spammers. This situation is an online arms race that will continue.

Gossip, Pass on and WOMBATs

Of all the animals of the world, humans are the greatest gossips. Gossip is a by-product of the unusually large human brain with its high-order faculty of language. The new millennium finds the human species with an extended global network backed by technology which makes for the ultimate pass on gossip system. Gossip, with satisfied customers, is what WOMBATs do. But always remember, unsatisfied customers gossip too!

100 Days

How to make a profit in 100 days

In the context of your own business or selling activities we can now focus on how you can make a profit in the next 100 days. When I work with my clients this is the newsell system that I use to help them multiply their sales activities by ten.

Think of your existing customers as only one tenth of your potential customers (those you don't yet have). You need to build your business by building your database of potential customers and by concurrently increasing the number of UNCHECKTOCHECKs you do each day.

To make a profit from newsell you need just three things:

1 an offer
2 a list
3 TT x 100 days.

An Offer

An offer is a BVS for your potential customers, usually a product or service, that gives them a much better outcome from their viewpoint, not yours. It's an offer to help them get a BVS in exchange for cash and one that requires either a YES or a NO answer. YES or NO are both viable answers, they are the normal business mixture. Collecting this mixture of YES or NO answers is how you escape from UNCHECK and the aim is to collect as much of this mixture as you can, ten times as many as at present.

In Australian Rules Football, there are only two ways to score – a goal or a behind. A goal is worth 6 points and a behind is worth 1 point. The team that has the biggest collection of goals and points wins. During the game players are either having a shot at goal or not. When they're not having a shot at goal they have no hope of scoring – they are in UNCHECK. When they are having a shot at goal they are in CHECK and they are building their collection of goals and points.

In newsell, when you go from UNCHECK TO CHECK you either get a YES or a NO. Let's say that a YES is worth 6 points and a NO is worth 1 point. Usually, the salesperson with the biggest collection of YESs and NOs wins. When they are in UNCHECK they have no hope of scoring, when they switch from UNCHECKTOCHECK they are building their collection of YESs and NOs.

How do you make an offer? You make your offer by flipping the UNCHECKTOCHECK newsell switch and you can try to collect at least 10 points a day. For example:

- 2 x YES = 12 points, or
- 1 x YES + 4 x NO = 10 points, or
- 15 x NO = 15 points.

There are many other possible combinations for scoring points.

A List

The fundamental unit of business is a customer and our most valuable business asset is our list of customers. This is our database. The most profitable of all customers are satisfied, repeat, long-term customers, sometimes known as 'registered users' – those customers whose names and addresses we have in our database. A traditional registered user is: a customer name and address. An online registered user is: a customer name and email address. Your objective is to look for ways to double the size of your database of registered users, both traditional and online.

Your database is a list of people for you to switch from UNCHECKTOCHECK. This list enables you to escape from UNCHECK. To build your list you'll need to spend some UNCHECK time to constantly feed names into this database of registered users, both traditional and online.

TT x 100 Days

This is the daily management part of your profit engine, and the most important part of your business. Every day you keep two measurements, your TT. You first measure the number of UNCHECKTOCHECK switches you think you will make tomorrow (this is a soft guess). Next, you measure the number of UNCHECKTOCHECK switches you actually made today (this is a hard fact).

HOW TO MAKE A PROFIT IN 100 DAYS!

1 Do you have an offer?
2 Do you have a database?
3 Have you kept your TT measurements for 100 days?

When you can answer YES to each of these questions you will already be making a profit. In the next few chapters we'll look at these three items – offer + database + TT – in more detail.

The Database

Names. Names. Names.
And, more names.

Your database is just a list of names. It's the list of names of potential customers you can contact about your offer. Even the phone book is a database, but perhaps your database is a little more qualified than that. How can you build your UNCHECKTOCHECK list? How can you build your database? There are just two questions I suggest my clients ask when building their database:

1 How many names do I currently have?
2 How can I multiply that number by ten?

Newsell does not rely on voodoo or miracles or 'closing techniques'. Newsell relies on science. So there is only one way to escape from UNCHECK and that is by making a CHECK move and to do that you need a name.

There are companies who are specialists in supplying lists of names, list brokers, and you can discuss your needs with them. But mostly, we can add names to our list on a daily basis as a normal part of our daily business activity.

Birds of a feather

You will have your own experience of how you choose a new name for your list but a good place to start is with your existing names. New customers are usually just like existing customers. As you think about the profile of your existing customers this can be a starting point (but not a restriction) for finding new names for your list.

There are many books that focus on this topic of database building and I think Tim Templeton's *The Referral of a Lifetime* (Berrett-Koehler, San Francisco, 2003) offers some very straightforward ideas. Also Wendy Evan's *How to Get New Business in 90 Days* (Millennium Books, Sydney, 1993) is a good one. Here are the sort of questions Wendy uses to build a database:

- Where are my current customers located?
- What industries are they in?
- What do I like about them?
- What do I dislike about them?

- Are they individuals or corporations?
- Are they big businesses or small businesses?
- Are they male or female or does it matter?
- What are they currently buying from me?
- How do they rate my offer?
- How do they rate my service?
- How often do I contact them?
- Do they Word of Mouth their own database?
- What customers have I lost in the last year?
- Who are my customers' competitors?

Word of Mouth

The most desirable way of adding names to your list is by Word of Mouth or WOM. This is sometimes called Buzz Marketing. WOM is when your *existing* customers tell someone on their own database about you and your offer. The psychology of buying is the psychology of trust. If your existing customer has a database of names and if what she says about you is credible, then this is WOM.

Example: Suppose you have ten customers. Suppose each of your customers has ten customers. If your customers were to tell their own databases about your offer then you are experiencing the benefits of WOM or Buzz.

This kind of replication is very powerful and is the basis of WOMBAT marketing or referral selling. A WOMBAT is a customer who becomes a virtual salesperson for an offer. They bought, they are happy, they tell others. This can only happen if the customer is very satisfied.

Many marketers use a reward or incentive to encourage a customer to WOM their offer but sometimes this backfires. Why? Because the new customer may not trust the referral. They may consider the referral is due more to the incentive and not to the quality of the offer.

WOMBAT marketing seeks to nurture customer trust. It requires clever thinking, expertise and experience.

WOMBAT and Viral Marketing

There is a distinction between WOM and WOMBAT which is worth mentioning here. The difference is: satisfaction. From a commercial business point-of-view, satisfaction is critical for profit.

Is it possible to be involved in WOM without being a satisfied customer? The answer is: Yes. For example, viral marketing can be an example of WOM where you don't need to be a satisfied customer to participate.

Most readers will have received an email from a friend with an audio or video attachment; usually an attention-getting, clever ad specifically made for spreading via email. They are often funny or shocking in some way and therefore have enough pass on value to get themselves replicated from database to database like a virus. I've received some really amusing ones and passed them on to appropriate friends. But, I was never a satisfied customer. I never bought the product and therefore I never told my friends about my satisfaction. The bottom line is that shareholders received no profit benefit from my participation.

Viral marketing is a fascinating development in darwinian marketing and the WWW is a haven for attention-getting viruses to be passed on from brain to brain via email. Clever creative people in ad agencies can make a name for themselves as viral marketers. However, that is not the same as WOMBAT marketing.

For an ad agency to become successful WOMBAT marketers they need to go beyond viral marketing and produce campaigns that create WOMBATs. This is a much more valuable skill because a WOMBAT has the added commercial advantage of being a paid-up and satisfied customer who is replicating other WOMBATs.

Viral, or WOM marketing may be useful for spreading brand recognition from database to database. WOMBAT marketing is useful for creating profit from database to database.

Brief your agency

I encourage my clients with big advertising budgets to include in their briefs to their agency a request for a WOMBAT marketing campaign. Agencies that are competent at WOMBAT marketing have a big advantage over those who can only do WOM campaigns.

> **Example:** Nudie, the Australian fruit juice company (even without the deep pockets of a Coke or Pepsi behind them) was recently voted one of the top ten brands in Australia. Tim Pethick, CEO, worked on a strategy of building a satisfying customer experience around Nudie. This experience helped create passionate customers, evangelists. Nudie uses events, sampling and word of mouth to create awareness. It's worth a visit to Nudie at www.nudie.com.au to see what they're doing.

Explore, with your agency, questions like:

- How can we create a WOMBAT marketing campaign?
- How can we measure the results of our WOMBAT campaign?
- How can we grow our WOMBAT database tenfold?
- How can we use customer feedback in our product design?
- How can we get daily customer feedback online?
- How can we work with bloggers and passion groups?
- How can we measure the ROI on our WOMBAT campaign?

- How can we get women talking about our product?
- How can we develop a B2B campaign for **WOMBATs.**
- What do we need to do to get started on a **WOMBAT** strategy?

Stealth marketing

There will always be tricksters, cheats, and the oldsell whatever-I-can-get-away-with merchants. For a good example of what WOMBAT marketing is NOT, contrast it with stealth marketing.

Where WOMBAT marketing relies on satisfied customers, stealth marketing relies on tricksters. Stealth marketing relies on paying people to say things that are not true or to misrepresent who they really are. This kind of espionage may have a place in James Bond movies but don't entrust your precious brand to stealth marketers and don't let them get anywhere near your future customers.

Using attractive but fake customers to prey on teenagers in bars to get them to buy the latest drink brand has recently made the headlines as an example of stealth marketing. Stupid. The infamous 'curiosity approach' used by stealth MLMers is another sad example of stealth marketing which has so backfired that the soap company has become known as 'the company that dare not speak its name'.

Business is about making a profit. The most profitable customers are those that are satisfied, repeat,

long-term buyers who then replicate. Short-term stealth
marketers who start off their relationship with a lie, just
don't get it!

Names x10

The bottom line is that adding names to your database is
a fundamental skill to practise on a daily basis. In
newsell, every day we practise using clever thinking,
experimentation and effort to explore ways to multiply
the number of names we have by ten.

In newsell, the one who has the most names wins!

The Offer

Is your offer A or B class?

A BVS is in the eye of the beholder

In my newsell seminars when I'm working with salespeople and their managers I often ask the following question: what were you before you became a salesperson? Eventually someone comes up with the answer I'm looking for: a customer!

So, take off your salesperson's hat for a moment and put on your customer's hat. As a customer, there are two classes of offers that come to your attention each and every day:

● B class: those offers that make it easy for you to say NO

● A class: those offers that make it easy for you to say YES.

Now put your salesperson's hat back on. No matter how much we are in love with our product nor how much our company raves about its service, when we get a NO it's usually because the customer sees it as a B class offer. If we want to design an A class offer then it must contain a BVS. The most important thing to bear in mind is that a BVS is in the eye of the beholder. In business, the beholder is the customer and the customer's viewpoint is what counts.

What is a BVS?

CVSTOBVS shows you how you can escape from your Current View of the Situation (CVS) to find a Better View of the situation (BVS), one which is ten times better! This is the basic School of Thinking brain software.

Instead of just using your brainpower to defend the 'rightness' of your CVS you can switch to using your brainpower to design or look for a BVS.

A BVS is ten times better than a CVS.

CVS = Current View of the Situation
TO = Now switch to
BVS = Better View of Situation.
BVS = CVS x 10

You can use the CVSTOBVS as a change switch. You can use it as brain software, to escape, to change, to explore, to learn, to create, to accelerate. You can use CVSTOBVS to escape from your CVS. CVSTOBVS is the 'value-added' role in the management process. With CVSTOBVS you can make decisions after you have explored options rather than before. CVSTOBVS can help solve problems and/or create opportunities. CVSTOBVS is a switch for change and is very useful in designing an offer for a customer. The important point to remember is the BVS is in the eye of the beholder.

Where's the BVS?

Selling is finding out what your customer's CVS is and then helping them get a BVS. An A class offer contains a BVS for your potential customers, usually a product or service that gives them a much better outcome from their viewpoint.

The customer might find a BVS in a more convenient way to order. A faster way to arrange delivery. A BVS might be a friendlier place to shop or much better after-sales-service. It might be better attention-getting packaging. Or, a less generic, more personalised offer. And so forth.

How do we know if the customer thinks our offer is a BVS? Ask them! That's what a CHECK move is for. Escape from UNCHECK and pick up the phone or send an email and make your offer.

An offer requires either a YES or a NO answer from your potential customer. YES or NO are both viable answers, they are the normal business mixture. We bank the YESs and the NOs are market research. The customers use NO to tell us (if we listen carefully) what we have to do to our offer, how we have to evolve it to get a YES. That's why NOs are so valuable in business.

Collecting this mixture of YES or NO answers is how you escape from UNCHECK and you aim to collect as much of this mixture as you can, ten times as much as you do currently.

How do you make an offer? You make your offer by flipping the newsell switch UNCHECKTOCHECK. The NO answers you get are valuable as feedback because they tell you that you have a B class offer. You use this valuable market research, these NO answers, to help evolve your offer from a B class offer to an A class offer. How can you tell when you have an A class offer? Your customers will tell you with a YES answer.

In other words, if you use the UNCHECKTOCHECK switch often enough to keep in contact with your potential customers they will teach you how to craft an offer that is easy for them to say YES. No closing technique on earth can beat this. When a customer says YES to an A class offer, closing techniques aren't needed. When a customer says NO to a B class offer, closing techniques aren't possible.

Newsell is all about escaping from UNCHECKTOCHECK with an A class offer and then doing this ten times more often. In contrast, oldsell is trying to use closing techniques to get customers to say YES to a B class offer. Customers hate oldsell. Customers like newsell. Customers punish oldsell by saying NO. Customers reward newsell by saying YES.

Flipping the Newsell Switch

Some of my favourite examples – old and new

Newsell rocks!

The promise of newsell is that it can produce sales results up to TEN TIMES those of oldsell because the focus is on the start and not on the close. The attention is on flipping the newsell switch from Uncheck to Check and doing it ten times more than ever before. UNCHECKTOCHECK X10.

Here are a few examples of my own, and others I have worked with over the years where we have flipped the switch and escaped from Uncheck with offers that then led to X10 results.

Thinking Instructors

In 1979 at JFK International airport in New York, I suggested to Edward de Bono that we should create 'thinking instructors' to teach thinking skills in schools, businesses and families around the world. Over the past 25 years this idea has grown to become the second largest program for the teaching of thinking in history. The Vatican's 500-year mission of exporting its own European thinking system (logic) is still far and away the largest ever.

GE X10

I've mentioned an example of working with GE earlier. I'll discuss it again here. I first met Jack Welch just after he became Chairman of the General Electric Company in the US. At a meeting in Marco Island, Florida in September 1984 I showed how he could use a strategy I called GE X10. At that time General Electric was a US$30-billion-dollar manufacturer, making everything from locomotives to light bulbs. GE was having the same sort of problem that most manufacturing companies were having at the time with shrinking markets and increasing competition.

The problem was: how do you get that unfair advantage when your competitors are doing the same as you are? At that time there was the quality drive; everyone was into 'quality'. Everyone was reading the same books, attending the same seminars, using the same consultants, doing the same thing, so there was a Red Queen effect – just like an arms race in biology. In Lewis Carroll's *Through the Looking Glass* the Red Queen had to run as fast as she could just to stay in the one place! Suppose you've got gazelles and you've got cheetahs. The genes in the cheetah pool are selected to make for faster running cheetahs in order to be able to catch the gazelles. At the same time, the gazelle gene pool is selecting for faster genes so gazelles can run faster to avoid being eaten – so you get this kind of genetic arms race. After all that effort you still get much the same number of cheetahs eating the same number of gazelles.

This is what was happening in manufacturing in the 1970s and '80s with arms races in 'quality' and 'excellence' and 're-engineering' and so on. Corporations in countries like the US and Australia were doing the same thing while competition was getting tougher, markets were shrinking and it was difficult to make that quantum leap. So, Jack was very interested in the concept of multiplying GE by ten. If you added a zero to GE, a $30-billion company, it would become a $300-billion company. He asked me to help him spread the GE X10 meme throughout the company which I did over the following 18 months. 'Finding a better way every day' became a GE slogan which was put up in every GE office and factory around the world.

By the time he retired, Jack Welch had switched GE from being a product-driven business bent on market share to a customer-driven business bent on profit share. In doing so, he grew GE from a $30-billion manufacturing company in 1985 to a clever $300-billion company in 1998. As a result, GE's shareholder value grew ten times making it the most valuable company in the world at the time.

AUSSIE BODIES X10

In October 2005, I ran another training program called Aussie Bodies X10 for a fast growing company in Port Melbourne. When I first was introduced to Aussie Bodies in 1993 (now at www.aussiebodies.com.au) it was a small Australian company that pioneered the use of protein as a food supplement for athletes and gyms. At that time, Maria Deveson, the CEO, and her devoted team were working hard to spread the 'protein idea' and to keep the small half-million-dollar company in a survival mode so it could live long enough to grow. She asked me about the newsell strategy. I trained the team in the newsell system and also became an equity investor. After a lot of hard work, Maria Deveson and her team have now grown Aussie Bodies to a $50-million-dollar enterprise with international distribution and a growing range of brands.

New York Hospitals

In 1979 I offered to show over 64 CEOs of New York hospitals how their own employees could come up with BVS ideas to cut costs in a 30-day lateral thinking campaign. My offer was presented to them at a lunch at the Waldorf-Astoria hotel which I hosted and included the offer of a full-page advertisement in *The New York Times* where they could brag to New Yorkers about the results of these efforts to reduce the cost of health-care and get good PR. Twenty-three hospitals signed up with a total of 41,000 employees participating. It was said in the media that this was the first time in New York's history that 23 hospitals had ever done *anything* together. Two television networks carried the story in their 6 pm news. In addition, *The New York Post*, the *Daily News*, several New York metropolitan newspapers, *Industry Week*, the *Wall Street Journal*, various magazines, industrial publications, and media around the country, in Europe, and even *The Herald* in Melbourne ran the story. According to the hospital CEOs, this PR aspect of the project alone made their efforts and their involvement worthwhile. To top it all off, there was $12 million in savings that the hospital employees generated during the lateral thinking campaign.

The Santa Barbara Learn-To-Think Project

In 1983, the City of Santa Barbara, 70 miles north of Los Angeles, received national attention by becoming the first community in the United States to 'teach itself to think'. The Santa Barbara Learn-To-Think Project involved educators, businesspeople, parents, legislators, community groups and children, all working together to teach themselves the skill of thinking. The project even received a special grant from the prestigious MacArthur Foundation.

In January 1983, I had suggested to a leading educator in Santa Barbara that if she could obtain signatures to the following letter from the mayor, the Chamber of Commerce, the superintendent of schools, the PTA, and other community leaders in Santa Barbara, then the School of Thinking would use publicity to promote the fact and officially declare Santa Barbara to be the first community in the United States ever to teach itself to think. The letter went as follows:

> Thinking has now become the fastest-growing industry in the United States. Of the 19 million new jobs created in the United States in the 1970s, 17 million jobs were in the thinking industry.
>
> The opportunity now exists for Santa Barbara to become the first community in the history of

the United States to teach itself to think. This project would involve leaders in Santa Barbara from education, business, community groups, parent groups and legislators. I support the Santa Barbara Learn-To-Think Project.

Signed: _____

Within ten days she produced letters signed by the mayor, the Chamber of Commerce, the superintendent of schools, the PTA and other community leaders. Since then, other communities and school districts around the world have begun projects to teach thinking to their constituencies.

ANZ Trustees

In February 1989, I showed ANZ Trustees how to replace their existing oldsell strategy with a newsell strategy for marketing their V2 Cash Common Fund. The two aims were to increase the number of new intermediary clients acquired and to increase the sales. We tracked the results for the first 12 months. Here are the results before newsell showing the year, the number of new intermediary clients and the sales. The middle column represents the number of new intermediaries (lawyers, accountants) added to their network and the right hand column represents the actual deposits into the V2 fund:

1986	34	$7 million
1987	39	$5 million
1988	38	$4 million

Here are the results *after* newsell

| 1989 | 161 | $70 million |

The results were in excess of TEN TIMES the previous results of oldsell.

CVS Review

How to find out what your customer REALLY wants

A problem well stated is a problem half solved

In this chapter we'll be talking about what I call the CVS Review. This is the theme of a meeting that you may want to have with a prospective customer as early in the relationship as possible ...

The Gallup Poll is one of the world's most credible organisations. It was founded by Professor George Gallup of Princeton who, as I've already mentioned, invented the use of the statistical sample in market research and opinion polling. This has so empowered public opinion that it may be the greatest act of democracy ever invented by a scientist. For his contribution, I always felt Dr Gallup deserved a Nobel Prize. He was also the originator of market research and, when he died in 1984, he was one of the pre-eminent marketing scientists in the world.

As my mentor, George was very keen for me to do two things: 1. encourage better use of our brains and 2. find ways to make better use of our experience. He felt the enormous intellectual capital reserves of the world were largely untapped. He said: 'Factors common to the successful can be identified as readily as those common to the unsuccessful' and that 'this is the simplest of all analytical processes and perhaps the most ignored in all departments of life'. His research showed that most of the problems facing individuals and nations on a daily basis have really already been solved but 'we make as little use of experience as we do of our brains'.

In other words, we are not very good at learning from each other. We all have to re-invent the wheel for ourselves. Even though solutions already exist for nearly all the problems we face each day, we are frequently victims of the NIH Syndrome (Not Invented Here). We tend to worry about fixing problems ourselves rather than searching for and identifying the solutions of others who have already solved similar problems.

Peer to Peer

Now that we have the Internet along with its search engines and intelligent agents we have an opportunity to learn and draw down from the whole world's experience, peer to peer. From the vast global reserves we can all make deposits and withdrawals of intellectual capital ... anyone, anywhere, anytime ... but only if we can escape from our own viewpoint. However, escaping from our CVS is one of the most difficult feats of thinking.

That is why George felt CVSTOBVS was such a useful switching method because it helped people to 1. identify a problem area (CVS) and 2. request a solution packet (BVS).

He impressed upon me the need to review the CVS of a customer before designing a BVS. He felt corporations and governments spent too little time reviewing the CVS of their stakeholders before offering them a BVS. In order to design a BVS from the customer's viewpoint you first have to pay attention to their CVS. This deliberate activity I call the CVS Review.

There is much research being conducted into brain activity in universities. For example, the Brain Sciences Institute at Swinburne University of Technology in Melbourne has a very promising technology for directly measuring the customer's CVS. In laboratory tests, brain activity is measured while people watch TV commercials and these tests have been successful in measuring the customer's CVS. However, there may be some time before these technologies get to the marketplace. Meanwhile, there is an easy method that anyone can use at any time to review the customer's CVS. It's called questions and answers, or ask and receive.

Two Ears and One Mouth

The simple skill of asking questions is widely underused, especially in selling. Oldsell has encouraged salespeople to use their 'gift of the gab' to tell customers what they need rather than to ask them what they want.

When I started out in the early 1970s my mentor, Fred Herman, along with Earl Nightingale, had written a book called *KISS: Keep It Simple Salesman*. Fred was best known for developing the skill of 'selling by asking questions'. He used to say, 'You've got two ears and one mouth so try using them in that proportion'.

Fred taught me his 7Q technique which I have evolved for reviewing a customer's CVS. It uses seven basic questions to review and explore the customer's CVS as a basis for helping them move to a BVS.

The 7 Question CVS Review – 7Q

Before jumping in with a solution for your customer you need to know what the problem is. This is not just your assumption of the problem but your customer's explicit CVS of the problem.

When you visit the GP she doesn't start off by selling you a cast for a broken leg. No. First, she asks you a series of questions. Based on your answers she may do further research and tests and consult colleagues. Eventually a diagnosis is reached and a treatment is prescribed.

You can do the same by asking these seven questions. This example was originally developed for selling insurance. I taught this to the AMP Moorabbin sales team in the 1970s and they rehearsed it so well that they became the number one insurance branch in the country in just 100 days.

This is a robust technique and one of the benefits of 7Q is that it can be remodelled to suit any selling situation for any product or service. If you decide to experiment with 7Q you will need to write and perfect your own version. It does pay to write it out and learn it like an actor learns lines. When you are skilled it will be second nature and spontaneous so you need to use your own idiom. Use the wording that is comfortable for you since you may not like some of the wording used here:

I don't know if I can help you or not but I called by to see if I can ... I guess you can't hate me for that, eh?

NO, I SUPPOSE NOT.

I just wanted to get your answer to a couple of questions, would you mind if I ask them?

OKAY

I've come to talk about insurance, but nobody wants to talk about insurance, do they? So let's not talk about insurance but I would like to discuss with you four quite important financial hazards that could be facing you about now. Would you be willing to spend a couple of minutes having a look at these four financial hazards?

IF 'YES' ... WRITE ON PAPER 1. 2. 3. 4. Well, there are four financial hazards which may be of importance to you also. They're these:

Number one is: Dying too soon. (write on paper)

Dying too soon is when your family needs to have a minimum income coming in on a monthly basis and if something were to happen to you and that income were no longer available to them, then I guess that would be a financial hazard, wouldn't it?

YES

Number Two is: Disability. (write on paper)

Disability is when your family still needs their monthly income but due to some accident to you it's no longer coming in, then that would be a financial hazard, huh?

Maybe there would even be some additional expenses for you too, so that could be a problem, couldn't it?

YES

Number Three is: Problem/Opportunity. (write on paper)

Money for a Problem or Opportunity is when maybe some time in your life a problem arises. Something unexpected, like an emergency and if you don't have money for this emergency then it's a financial hazard for you, isn't it? Or, maybe instead it's an unexpected opportunity. Something that you decide is really a great opportunity for you and your family, if only you had the money to take advantage of it. If you lose it because you don't have access to the necessary cash, then that too would probably be a financial hazard for you, do you agree?

YES

And finally, Number Four is: Living too long. (write on paper)

Living too long is when you do make it to retirement but you no longer have the energy or the inclination to earn a monthly income. However, you still need the money coming in for you and your family to enjoy your retirement. If that money isn't coming in for one reason or another, then I suppose that would be a real financial hazard for you, fair enough?

YES

Okay. Just suppose you could wave a magic wand right now and get the solution to only one of these hazards. Which one would you choose as

being the most important one to you right now . . .
Dying too soon? Disability? Money for a Problem
or Opportunity? or Living too long?

LIVING TOO LONG.

Really? Would that be more important than
Dying too soon?

YES

Would that be more important than
Disability?

YES

Would that be more important than money for
a Problem or Opportunity?

So it really is the Living too long?

YES IT IS.

May I ask why this is so important to you right
now?

WELL, XXXXXXXXXXXXXXXXX (here, customer
elaborates on his or her CVS).

And how does that make you feel? (open
question to encourage customer to discuss CVS)

XXX XXX XXX XXX XXX XXX

And then what happened? (open question to
encourage customer to discuss CVS)

XXXX XXX XXXX XXXX XXX XXX

Which means . . . ? (open question to
encourage customer to reveal CVS)

XXX XX XXXXX XXXX XXX XXX

And so what would you hope to achieve?
(open question for customer to discuss CVS)

XXX XXX XXXXXX XXX XXX XXX XXXXXX

Will that be your main priority? (open question for customer to discuss CVS)

XXXXX XXXX XXXX XXXXX

How does your wife/husband feel about this? (open question for customer to discuss CVS)

XXXXX XXX XXX XXXXX

Okay. Well, wow much would you need coming in each month to maintain your standard of living?

ABOUT $4500

Boy, you really do have a problem don't you? Looks like I got here just in time. You know, I was just wondering, how much would you be willing to put aside on a monthly basis to help solve this problem?

$150

Could you really do that? Every month, even when things are a bit tight?

YES, I COULD

Okay. Well, let's see how much of your problem we can solve for $150 a month.

(NOW, GET OUT RATE BOOK AND DESIGN A BVS FOR $150 OR LESS)

7Q Tips

If you want to use this strategy successfully to help customers discuss their CVS you need to be low-key and natural. To do this you need to work at it and here are some tips that I've found helpful:

1. Experiment with this at least ten times with potential customers and listen to their comments carefully. Your customers are the best teachers on how to evolve this technique.
2. Rewrite your final version and then, like a professional actor, learn your 7Q 100 per cent Shakespearean word perfect.
3. Think about the benefits of being skilled at the CVS Review.
4. Become so expert on this technique that it is second nature and spontaneous.
5. Be willing to spend around 25 hours of practice, repetition and rehearsal on 7Q over the next 30 days.
6. Make it fun to do and enjoy the process.
7. Help one another, work with your team and don't rest until every member of your team has become comfortably expert at this.
8. Think up new and creative ways to enjoy the rehearsals.
9. Pay particular attention to the open questions that encourage the customer to discuss their CVS. Listen! Listen! Listen to what your customer says.
10. Help them get what they want by designing a BVS around your product or service.

The Message

The message is the medium

In one form or another, life has existed on earth for over 3500 million years. Neural nets – conscious neural networks – like those in your brain, are a comparatively recent innovation and arose about 60 million years ago. The rapid expansion in size of the human brain has occurred only over the last few million years due to the pressures of survival in the arms race of brain against brain.

Humans with lesser brains could not survive as well as those who had more complex brains. Therefore those brains with better memories, better strategies and greater flexibility were naturally selected. They survived long enough to replicate and pass their genes on to the next generation. Those that didn't survive long enough to replicate were not selected.

We no longer hunt or live in caves. Science and technology, products of our enlarged brains, our neural nets, have overtaken evolution. We now drive intelligent cars that use satellites to know where they are, and we live in smart-wired buildings with automatic climate control that moderates temperature whether we live in a desert or on top of a mountain.

Communication

The Scientific Revolution started about three hundred years ago. Seventeenth-century thinkers built their ideas on the works of early Greek thinkers all the way back to Democritus who put forward the theory of the atom and Pythagoras who put forward the theory of the kosmos. But it was the invention of the printing press by Gutenberg and others that allowed scientists to communicate more easily with each other. Brain to brain. Neural net to neural net. Nothing spurs intellectual development like an improvement in communications! Only about 1000 books a year were produced in Europe before 1500. By 1950 this number had risen to 120,000 a year!

Then, in 1969 the US-based Defence Advanced Research Projects Agency (DARPA) made a fateful decision in human evolution. They realised that it was possible to take a quantum leap in communications between their scientists and researchers based at different geographical locations. They networked (joined by telecommunication) four large computers and established DARPANET. This had grown to 37 networked computers by 1972 and the name evolved to ARPANET. In addition to exchanging boring (but no doubt important) military information the users on the ARPANET began sending each other personal messages by electronic mail – email – and that's when the communications big bang took off.

Communication: computer to computer

By 1987, any educational facility – academic, military, government – could use the network in any country allied to the US. Scientists could now exchange scientific papers across the world in milliseconds. If these developments are startling, they seem sluggish when compared to the speed and acceleration of the knowledge explosion. The Information Revolution is less than 60 years old. A single BMW car today has more computing power than the whole world had 60 years ago. Your iPod has more memory than the computers that took the first rocket to the moon!

Communications facilitates intellectual growth and the generation of information. People use iPods to swap whole libraries of music and other digital information (mine can hold 30,000 tunes but so far I've only got 3000). Anyone can use their desktop computer for self-publishing, editing movies, blogging their opinions to the world – for creating and webcasting their own content.

All this information is exchanged at the speed of light and the slowest link in the chain is now you, the human being!

Communication: computer net to computer net

Meanwhile, in 1990, ARPANET evolved into the INTERNET, the network of networks and with the subsequent arrival of the World Wide Web, the Net, as we know it, is now available to anyone with a computer and a modem to connect in to it. The number of users has grown from 5000 to over a billion in a decade.

Increasingly, we are doing all of the above on our handheld device. Our mobile phone, iPod and computers are all converging into the newest communication tool for our big human brain.

Looking at the Net and the World Wide Web and its extraordinary growth we can notice and focus upon a powerful and useful unit of measurement. What do you think it might be?

It's a fundamental unit of measurement on the Internet/WWW and I believe it's also the fundamental unit of measurement in business, especially in newsell.

The Message

When it comes to intellectual capital, the message is the medium. The message is THE most fundamental unit of intellectual capital. I believe that the message is about to take a quantum leap and that we are on the threshold of a whole new appreciation of its importance in the business context.

Technology has now elevated the message, as a unit of measurement, to the level of other basic business measurements like dollars and personnel. I believe that, before too long, measuring messaging in a business will become a daily protocol. I believe that the introduction of this daily measurement – counting the messages – will directly lead to immediate and significant increases in productivity and profitability. I believe that the message is becoming the most important unit of measurement on the Internet.

What is a message?
Our trusty old Oxford English Dictionary tells us that a message is an oral or written communication sent by one person to another. I think this is fine, as far as it goes, but now it's time to take it a little further. It's useful to look at a message in the light of the full potential of its consequences – the reply.

Just as psychologists study messages in a behavioural context and look at both the STIMULUS and the RESPONSE, in a business context we want to look at both the MESSAGE and the REPLY. So, in messaging, there are two parts we are interested in: MESSAGE IN and also MESSAGE OUT. We also need to pay attention to what happens between the two.

Introducing MiMo

To help the message (and messaging) achieve its potential in the brave new world of business cybertransactions I am putting forward a new unit of measurement called MiMo.

Mi is a message in and Mo is a message out.

Mi is an information stimulus received and Mo is an information response given out. You receive a Mi and you send back a Mo. Together they make up a MiMo. No doubt you have seen how this works in a wide range of business applications and, of course, we use this format in a deliberate way in School of Thinking on-line training courses with our daily breadmails (MO) and Feedback Questions (MI).

The Message Switch: Message-in to Message-out

I have written often enough about the usefulness of the SWITCH as a model. There are the two positions as in ON to OFF or FLIP to FLOP or CVS to BVS or UNCHECK to CHECK. In messaging we can also use the Message Switch: Mi to Mo or MiMo.

MiMo examples:

● Just now, a sudden burst of positive electricity from a neighbouring nerve cell was received by a particular neuron in your brain. Then that neuron fired up and sent a similar message out along its axon to its next door neighbour = MiMo.

- Last night a young mother heard her baby cry out, she turned over and said to her husband, 'Your turn, darling' = MiMo.
- This morning an email was received by a White House aide. The aide checked her files and then sent a new message to her boss = MiMo.
- Yesterday a patient received a phone call from his dentist's office confirming today's appointment. He agreed he'd be there for his 0930 appointment and so this morning he showed up on time = MiMo.
- Your server sends a message and your PC replies = MiMo.
- Tomorrow a stewardess on a jumbo jet will see a light and hear a *ping* showing that the passenger in seat 4A needs attention. She will switch off the light and greet her passenger by his name = MiMo.
- Two thousand years ago, a gladiator, with his foot on the throat of his opponent and his short sword poised for the kill, looks up at the thumbs of the spectators = MiMo.
- In a few years time, over a million viewers of a national TV program will respond to a prime minister's televised speech by pressing a button on their interactive device. He will change his policy as a result of considering their feedback = MiMo.

● A few minutes ago a customer walked into a store near you. The salesperson immediately said to the customer, 'Can I help you?' The customer replied, 'No thanks, just looking!' and immediately walked out of the store = MiMo.

The MiMo idea is the basis of newsell and it's also how the UNCHECKTOCHECK switch works.

Bonus 250 switches

As a bonus, at the end of this book, I've included a sample of 250 UNCHECKTOCHECK switches you can use to get a response from your customers. These examples are all Mi's and the response you get from your customers are the Mo's.

Newsell is about ways and systems you can use to MIMO X10 – to multiply your Mis and Mos by ten.

The Next 10 Days

Time to cut bait or start fishing

Most new programs fail, not because they didn't finish but because they didn't even get started. Here we will focus on what you can do to get started with using newsell to grow your own business.

Yes, it's hard to get started. That's why, in newsell, we put the emphasis on the start rather than the close. Indeed, the whole premise of newsell is that 99 per cent of sales are lost, not at the close but at the start. Or, in newsell speak, 99 per cent of UNCHECKTOCHECK switches have yet to be flipped!

In this chapter we focus on the next ten days as a simple way to get you started.

Getting Started with TTs

TT: This is the daily management and most important part of your business. Every day you keep two measurements, your TTs for Today and Tomorrow. You first measure the number of UNCHECKTOCHECK switches you know you made Today (the last 24 hours) and this is a fact. Next, you measure the number of UNCHECKTOCHECK switches you think you will make Tomorrow (the coming 24 hours) and this is just a guess.

By the way, the two numbers don't have to match up. TTs are definitely *not* goal-setting although some managers misunderstand the use of TTs as such. TTs are simply using feedback to monitor your progress. TTs are a way of developing the mental skill of being able to measure and project every day. The main purpose of TT training is to develop, in your own brain, the twin business skills of measuring and projecting.

TTs may seem a bit awkward at first but if you are patient and persevere with these TTs for just one week you will get used to them and then TTs will be a skill you will have for the rest of your career. Few people can do this on a daily basis. If you can do them, TTs WILL help you build your monthly commissions.

NOTE: It's easy to assume that TTs are the familiar motivational tool of goal-setting so I'll repeat the warning here: TTs are NOT goal-setting.

The 'push/pull' motivational concepts are old (though longevity does not necessarily mean they are ineffective) but to say that is what we are promoting in TT training is to miss the point. TTs are not being used as push/pull 'motivational' goal-setting. They are not motivational but cybernetic. They are to help people develop the two cognitive skills of 'noticing feedback' and 'projecting forward'.

This intention is evidenced by the fact that there is not (or should not be) any management discussion of the actual numbers in the TTs. No typical comments like, 'You said you'd do 3/4 and you only did 2/1.' No remarks like, 'John did 8/8 and is the best one in the team' and so forth. 0/0 is quite okay in this system.

These differences between the application of the push/pull motivational model and the start/do/notice/ think cybernetic model also produce, as one would expect, quite different consequences in behaviour and results.

In practical terms, it will take some time and practice for you and your team to learn these skills, to see the results and to gain confidence in them. An expectation of 100 days to achieve a cultural change is realistic. In my consulting practice I discuss this with management and I stick with the team by providing daily training for that period. Whether or not an individual or team is willing to continue is up to them. Our previous patterns of expectation often defeat our ability to change our habits of thinking.

There's another interesting feature of TTs compared to goal-setting and more traditional forms of management. As I mentioned above, zeros are okay! Yep, it's true. Nothing is no problem. Whenever you put 0 under Tomorrow or 0 under Today, it's good. Why? Because the success of this system is due to the process of keeping daily measurements not on the actual measurements themselves. So, you succeed when you record a zero in TTs you only fail when you make no record at all.

Instructions for starting:

1 Use the next page or make a copy of it.
2 Under DATE record today's date.
3 Under TODAY record accurately the number of times you switched from UNCHECKTOCHECK in the last 24 hours.
4 Under TOMORROW record your guess of the number of times you will flip the UNCHECKTOCHECK switch tomorrow (next 24 hours). Remember, this is not a goal, just a guess.
5 Repeat steps 2–5 for the next ten days.

THE NEXT TEN DAYS STARTING TODAY:
(TODAY'S DATE)

TODAY   TOMORROW

1 _____

2 _____

3 _____

4 _____

5 _____

6 _____

7 _____

8 _____

9 _____

10 _____

The Next 100 Days

The Newsell Coaching Program

'The essence of strategy is to train day and night.'
– Miyamato Musashi, *Book of Five Rings*

If you've completed the experiment in the previous chapter, then you are already on your way. You can continue on for the first 100 days which is not much more than a business quarter. In my experience, any business growth idea that is worth doing at all is usually worth doing for at least one business quarter.

Record your daily TTs for the next 100 days. You don't have to concern yourself with 'closing the sale'. Just manage your UNCHECKTOCHECK switches and measure them daily and TCB (take care of business) with of those who are interested. Do this and you will have your own newsell system up and running.

If you are a salesperson, you can operate this system on your own initiative. Alternatively, why not do it with your team? Get your manager to assist you with his or her experience, recognition and support. If you are an MLMer you can use this system and teach it to your downline. If you are a small business person, you and your partner or your associates can do this together.

People in non-profit situations such as charities can also use this system effectively. Be creative and make it fun but be disciplined about doing your TTs daily.

By the way, anyone can do this. You don't have to be a 'salesperson'. In my clients' businesses we have people in the storeroom, people in manufacturing, people in R&D, people in accounts all using newsell. In fact, anyone, anywhere, anytime can use newsell.

There's really nothing to stop you carrying out this experiment and I've also supplied a collection of 250 UNCHECKTOCHECK switches for you to play with. Just choose the ones you like. Many of them you can use to TCB – take care of business.

Operating instructions for your newsell system:

1 Start now!
2 Record the number of UNCHECKTOCHECK switches you did today.

3 Guess and record the number of UNCHECKTOCHECK switches you might do tomorrow.

4 Repeat steps 2 and 3 for the next 100 days.

Newsell Coaching

If you don't want to do this by yourself but you want assistance, coaching and daily encouragement for the next 100 days then you can go to www.newsellcoaching.com and enroll yourself and if you are a sales manager or business owner, you can also enroll your sales team.

Go and Talk to the WOMBATS

As a bonus, here are 250 UNCHECKTOCHECK switches. They are things you can say to the WOMBATs. They are phone calls you can make to WOMBATs and messages you can send out to them. These are randomly selected from my collection of over 800. Any one of these can be used for doing Mos (Message Outs).

1 Market research shows that the third most powerful way to talk to a WOMBAT is by a personal email. If you are using a points system, this is one point.

2 The second most powerful way to talk to a WOMBAT is by personal phone call. This is two points.

3 The most powerful way to talk to a WOMBAT is face to face because the research shows that this is the medium that WOMBATs prefer. Take three points.

Some of these 250 work better by phone or voicemail, others by postmail or email and most work well in scheduled or unscheduled meetings. Adapt them to suit your offer you are currently working with.

Most of the time I prefer questions. Questions get you started and are the ideal UNCHECKTOCHECK switch. WOMBATs like to be asked questions. You can ask a question then you listen carefully to what the WOMBAT has to say and then you can ask the next question. While you cannot control the answers, you can always control the questions and that's enough to make the question a classic UNCHECKTOCHECK switch.

Most of them are examples of questions that you can use to get the attention of your potential customer, to make an offer, to follow up, to stay in contact, to provide service, to review their CVS, to help evolve your offer from B class to A class and most of all, to escape from UNCHECK.

Some of these questions you can use just as they are. Others will require some remodelling to suit your unique situation. Some I like and some I don't like. Some you will like, others you won't like. Start with the ones you like then gradually widen your repertoire by experimenting with new ones.

George Gallup once told me that business was the ultimate laboratory. Every day there are new customers and new situations with which to experiment. Don't be afraid of making mistakes. Remember, the newsell strategy seeks to generate a mixture of YES and NO answers, and then gradually growing that mix ten times. Lastly, if you are a manager, try and make it fun and don't DYSH your salespeople!

250 UNCHECKTOCHECK Switches

Do you ever lose sleep worrying about ...?

How many times have you unexpectedly run out of ...? (Sent letter with catalog)

If you sent in (the application) would you sleep better tonight?

What if you no longer had to put up with (back pain)?

Do you waste valuable time (keeping schedules up to date)?

Did you know that you can harm (your dog by bathing him)?

Did you lose money (trying to collect bad debts)?

You can knock ten strokes off your golf game by (subscribing to *NewGolf*)!

When you (subscribe) you get (a dozen free golf balls!)

Did you ever think you would find out how to ...

Since you are looking for ways to save money, shall I show you how to cut your (meeting) costs by at least 25 per cent?

Since cutting costs is important to you, would you like to see how to slash your next (training) budget by 20 per cent, while at the same time increasing sales by 50 per cent?

If you really want to reduce costs are you willing to ...?

It looks like costs are your major consideration so let's look at this (model).

On the phone you said you had no money for this, what if it didn't cost you a penny?

Is being able to save $10,000 during the next fiscal year of interest to you?

If you could find a way of making an extra $1000 by Friday, guaranteed, would you act on it?

If you knew you would find a way of really impressing your boss would you watch this video?

Have you ever seen a (meeting) idea that just totally blew your socks off? Well, get ready ...!

Would you like to see something that is so exciting it will keep you awake tonight?

What would it take to really amaze you? Well, get ready ...?

Are you sitting down? Well get ready for some very exciting news! Are you ready?

Let me ask you this? Do you have a lot of willpower? Well, you'd better have! When you see this video you will get an irresistible urge to ...!

Have you ever seen anything like this before?

Who else, other than yourself, should see this demonstration?

Are those your children? What are their ages?

These are handsome plants ... how do you keep them in such great shape?

Your people here seem so happy. What's your secret to keeping them so motivated?

It amazes me that you keep your desk so clean! What's your secret?

What is it that you most like about your job here?

Your company has an interesting name. Can you tell me the history of that name?

Could you tell me how you manage to keep calm under these trying circumstances?

Is that your golfing trophy? What did you shoot to win?

I don't know if you realise how much is at stake for your company but ...?

How many times during the day do you look at yourself in the mirror?

What do we have to do now to make you completely happy?

What would happen to the productivity of your sales team if you didn't have this (meeting)? Why?

Since you are looking for increased sales, watch this!

Since you are looking for ways to increase sales, shall I show you how to boost your (sales calls) by at least 25 per cent?

If you really want more sales are you willing to ...?

Since it looks like sales are your major consideration so let's look at this (copy).

Do your customers deserve this?

Would you like to see how to double those results?

If you were one of your customers, and you could have (A) or (B), which would you go for? Why?

Since your customers are so important to you, would you like to see how you can exceed their expectations on this?

Since you mentioned the importance of 'Quality', tell me what you think of this?

Do you think your customers would appreciate this quality?

'I'd like to place a person-to-person call to ...!'

In a recent survey, our customers claimed that we increased their (collection of delinquent accounts) by 30 per cent. Perhaps we can do the same for you.

Would you like to escape to tropical Antigua for six relaxing days and five exciting nights as our special guest?

P.S. When you call ask for your two free tropical T-shirts you can wear on the beach!

Do you have spare time to earn a part-time income?

Would you like to learn a new income skill from experts ...?

There are six easy steps for turning your PC into a money-making part-time business. Would you like to know what they are?

Would you like further information on this – it's free?

Did you get your free ...?

I'm calling to check that you received the information you asked for?

Is there anything we forgot to send you?

I received your letter today and I'm calling to say that the information you asked for is on its way.

How many times have you unexpectedly run out of (batteries)?

Thanks for your interest in the (Aqua Inflatable Raft).

Can you guess how long it takes to inflate? Two minutes!

Would a 30-day free trial be of interest to you?

Would a 'buy-today' discount be of interest to you?

You can save the whale from extinction!

Are you aware of what's happening to . . . ?

If tonight's news showed your home burning down, would you be able to replace the valuable personal and financial documents that you'd lose?

To find out more today call our toll free 008 number . . .

Ask for a free (photo inventory of your household possessions) when we meet.

Would you like us to do a free survey of your (filing system)?

Your neighbour said you might want to know about our Green Green Lawn Service, is now a good time?

Your neighbour's now paying less for his lawn service . . .

Your competitor has lowered his purchasing price . . .

You can pay much less that that for even better service!

Would you like a free estimate?

Your catalog gave me an exciting idea for increasing sales . . .

TAX ALERT! TAX ALERT! TAX ALERT!

The new tax law can cut your salary by 30 percent this year.

Do you know how to protect yourself from this?

You must be quick off the mark if you want this (benefit).

Would you like to run a pilot to see how it works?

Have you tasted this?

I think this may interest you also!

Did (Name) give you one of these to try?

Do you believe in the saying 'If at first you don't succeed, try, try again'? I do and that's why I'm writing to you again about ...

I was very impressed with the way your people answer the telephone ...

Three weeks ago you bought our ...

How long will your current supplies last?

What will you do then?

Thank you.

Happy Birthday!

Happy Christmas!

Happy New Year!

Happy Chanukah!

Congratulations.

I'm sorry to hear ...

Bon voyage!

Good Luck.

I read about your new acquisition, congratulations.

Happy Anniversary.

Four weeks ago you may have made a mistake. Luckily there's still time to fix it!

What do you want to tell them?

Why do you think she wants it?

Who else do you think will use it?

How do you think she will use it?

How long has she been looking for ... ?

What does she want to accomplish?

Who told you about ... ?

What was it about our (product) that you really liked?

What else did you like?

And then what happened?

And what did (they) say then?

How did that make you feel?

And what did you decide to do next time?

Why is that so important to you?

Boy, you really did have a blast, didn't you?

By the way, who do you know who would enjoy this?

And what did Mr (Your Boss) say about that? etc.

Just suppose we could (do A), would you then (do B)?

Mr (name), why are you putting all this pressure on me?

Is this the best you can do right now?

What is the alternative to this?

What other choice do you have?

What else do you feel is possible here?

You really cannot see any other possibilities?

In other words, you feel ... !

What is your (wife's) point-of-view?

Have you considered your customer's reaction to this?

What do you feel will be your partner's point-of-view?

Is this a big problem right now?

Do you see a way to overcome it?

What question can you ask me now?

Which means ...?

And ...?

When you say 'unhappy', Anne, what does that mean?

If she won't agree, what then?

What important factor have we not considered?

What else?

Is this a plus or a minus for you?

What do you find most interesting about this?

How could we turn this into a plus?

Are you sure this is a minus?

What are you hoping to achieve?

What is you main objective here?

Is that your aim?

This will have immediate consequences, what are they likely to be?

What will be the long-term consequences of this?

If you go ahead this year, what will be the consequences for (next year)?

What will be the negative consequences of this?

What will be the positive result of this move?

Is this your main priority right now?

What is your main priority?

What is Mr (Your Boss's) top priority?

What is your lowest priority now?

Can you see any other disadvantages to this?

What is the main advantage to you on this?

Could this move lead to an even better position?

Is this judgement based on the value of the idea or on his emotions at the present?

Have you explored both sides of this proposal?

Have you reached your decision yet?

Has she made a choice yet?

Whose advice can you get on this?

What have we left out?

How will this affect your union representative?

Does your (husband) share your goal?

What help can he give you?

How can we break this down into smaller, easier, objectives?

Which objective is the most important, (A or Z)?

Why have you chosen this as your priority now?

Can we come back to this later?

Did you ask your people for their ideas?

Why not?

What other method have you considered?

If you weren't satisfied, what would you do?

What word best describes this kind of situation?

What would your (customer) select from these?

What's another way of looking at this situation?

What is the very first thing to do now?

What is the first step to take now?

How shall we start this?

When can we get started?
What do we need to get started?
How shall we tackle this?
What is the best way to organise this situation?
Let's focus on (part B) now?
What are we focusing on now?
Shall we switch our focus on to ...?
What is the next point we should focus on?
What has been achieved so far?
Can you sum up what we've got so far?
Let's consolidate! Where are we with this situation?
What have we done and what is still left?
What can we conclude from all this information?
What is your feeling now?
Is there any conclusion we can make yet?
What are we blind to here?
Is this a fact or an opinion?
Is this good enough to use as evidence?
What are the areas of agreement?
What are the areas of disagreement?
What label can we give to this?
Could this be an exaggeration?
Could we be wrong?
If this were wrong, how could we tell?
What would it mean if we were wrong?
How can we tell?
Can we brainstorm this for a minute?
Why not?
What are we taking for granted here?

How can we challenge this?

What is dominating this situation?

How can we escape from this?

What is the main fault with this idea?

How can we remove it?

Can we combine (P) with (Q)?

Does this fit with the requirements?

Does this meet with the specifications?

If you made a guess, what would it be?

What do you suppose it might be?

What is the primary target here?

What result do you want from this?

What input do we need now?

What is the traditional solution for this?

What other solutions are there?

What action needs to be taken now?

What is the action step?

Before we begin could you outline how your situation has changed since our last meeting?

Can we start by reviewing what we need to get accomplished before we leave today?

I have made an agenda, may I show it to you?

Obviously you are pressed for time. What would you like to get out of this meeting?

Which of these three main points is critical for you?

My real reason for coming here today is to find out how to get you back as a satisfied customer. Is that a fair enough goal?

We really appreciate you coming to (Our Company). What made you decide to give us the opportunity to bid?

Ideally, what would you hope to accomplish from coming here?

Looks like you got here just in time, doesn't it?

How much in a hurry are you?

I was wondering about your timetable? What are the steps you went through last time you (did this)?

What are your expectations in terms of (time)?

What other (Companies) have you considered?

Do we have any competition at this time?

Is any one else bidding for this?

What do we have to do now to make you completely happy?

What do you want (your people) to say about this (meeting)?

Thank you for letting me know that you placed your order for (packaging) with another company.

Summary

Newsell is digital selling. It's darwinian marketing. In newsell there are only two positions – UNCHECK and CHECK. These two possible digital states – UNCHECK or CHECK – are what is known as the Newsell Switch. Just like the electron switch that can change from 0 to 1 or from 1 to 0, this digital Newsell Switch can change from UNCHECKTOCHECK or from CHECK to UNCHECK.

Operation of the Newsell Switch from UNCHECKTOCHECK is denoted by the symbol:

UNCHECKTOCHECK

Management of this switch is what newsell is all about. By the time you have read this book you will hopefully be clear about the UNCHECKTOCHECK switch and how you can immediately use it to increase growth in your business.

How powerful is your growth engine? . . .
Can you raise profits this quarter by 10 per cent? 20 per cent? 30 per cent? 40 per cent? . . .
You can if you've got a newsell system!
How? A newsell system boosts your profit by immediately *doubling* the sales activity of your business. It allows you to focus on prospecting for new names and checking them with better offers. This gives you the market presence of a much faster growing enterprise!

When your business runs a newsell system you get:

UNCHECKTOCHECK – more prospectors in your team
UNCHECKTOCHECK – more prospecting hours each
day/week
UNCHECKTOCHECK – more proactive prospecting
UNCHECKTOCHECK – more prospecting skills

UNCHECKTOCHECK – more accurate prospecting
measurement
UNCHECKTOCHECK – more daily prospecting control
UNCHECKTOCHECK – more prospecting experiments
and ideas
UNCHECKTOCHECK – more individual prospects –
quantity
UNCHECKTOCHECK – more qualified prospects – quality
UNCHECKTOCHECK – more satisfied customers
UNCHECKTOCHECK – more referrals
UNCHECKTOCHECK – more WOMBATS, word-of-mouth
marketers
UNCHECKTOCHECK – more successful salespeople
UNCHECKTOCHECK – stronger market position
UNCHECKTOCHECK – more profits.

Bibliography

Ackoff, Russel L, *Redesigning the Future*, New York: John Wiley, 1974

Albrecht, Karl, *At America's Service*, Homewood, Ill: Dow Jones-Irwin, 1988

American Marketing Association, Definition of Terms, Chicago, 1961

Aunger, Robert, *The Electric Meme: A New Theory of How We Think*, New York: The Free Press, 2002

Barber, Richard, *The Knight and Chivalry*, New York: Harper Colophon, 1970

Blakemore, Colin, *Mechanics of Mind*, London: Cambridge University, 1977

Bowler, Peter, *The True Believers*, Sydney: Methuen, 1986

Bradford, Ernle, The Great Siege: Malta 1565, New York: Penguin, 1964

Branden, Nathaniel, *Honoring the Self*, New York: Bantam, 1985

Branson, Richard, *Losing My Virginity: The Autobiography*, Sydney: Random House, 2002

Brenner, Reuven, *Betting On Ideas*, Chicago: University of Chicago, 1989

Brockman, John, *The New Humanists: Science at the Edge*, New York: Barnes & Noble, 2003

Byrd, Richard F, *Guide to Personal Risk-Taking*, New York: AMACOM, 1974

Calder, Nigel, *The Mind of Man*, London: BBC, 1970

Canfield, B.R., *Salesmanship: Practices and Problems*, New York: McGraw-Hill, 1958

Catalogue of the Records of the Order of St. John of Jerusalem, Malta, 1964

The Dalai Lama, *My Land and My People*, London: Weidenfeld & Nicolson, 1962

Davies, Paul, *The New Physics*, Cambridge UK: Cambridge University Press, 1989

Davies, Roger H. B., *PawTalk: A Guide For Getting What You Want*, Toronto: Springboard Books, 2004

Dawkins, Richard, *Blind Watchmaker*, New York: Norton, 1987
    A Devil's Chaplain, London: Wiedenfeld & Nicolson, 2003
    The Ancestor's Tale: A Pilgrimage To The Dawn of Life, London: Weidenfeld & Nicolson, 2004

de Bono, Edward, *The Five-Day Course in Thinking*, New York: Basic Books, 1968
    The Mechanism of Mind, New York: Simon & Schuster, 1969
    Lateral Thinking: A Textbook of Creativity, New York: Harper & Row, 1970
    The Greatest Thinkers, New York: Putnam, 1976
    Teaching Thinking, London: Temple Smith, 1976

de Bono, Edward, and Hewitt-Gleeson, Michael, *The Learn-To-Think Coursebook*, Santa Barbara: CAPRA/NEW, 1983

De Rosa, Peter, *Vicars of Christ*, London: Bantam, 1988

Dent, Harry S., *The Next Great Bubble Boom*, New York: Simon & Schuster, 2005

Diagram Group, *Comparisons*, New York: St. Martin's, 1980

Dichter, Ernest, *Handbook of Consumer Motivation*, New York: McGraw-Hill, 1964

Edwards, Paul and Sarah, *Making Money in Cyberspace*, New York: Tarcher Putnam, 1998

Ernest, John W., and Ashman, Richard D., *Selling Principles and Practice*, New York: McGraw-Hill, 1979

Fay, Allen, *Making Things Better by Making Them Worse*, New York: Hawthorn, 1976

Feldman, Ben, *Creative Selling*, Rockville Centre, New York: Farnsworth, 1974

Fischer, Louis, *The Essential Gandhi*, New York: Vintage, 1962

Fox, Jeffrey J., and Gregory, Richard C., *The Dollarization Discipline*, Hoboken: John Wiley & Sons, 2004

    How To Become A Rainmaker, Sydney: Random House, 2000

Funk, Robert W., and Hoover, Roy W., *The Five Gospels: What Did Jesus Really Say?* New York: Macmillan, 1993

Gallup, George, *The Miracle Ahead*, New York: Harper & Row, 1964

Girard, Joe, *How to Sell Anything to Anybody*, New York: Simon & Schuster, 1971

Godin, Seth, *Survival Is Not Enough*, New York: The Free Press, 2002

Greenberg, Herbert, *The Successful Salesman*, New York: Auerbach, 1972

Greenleaf, Robert K., *Teacher as Servant*, New York: Paulist, 1979

Gribbin, John, *In Search of the Double Helix*, New York: Bantam, 1985

Herman, Fred, *Selling Is Simple*, New York: Vantage, 1979

Herman, Fred and Nightingale, E., *"KISS: Keep It Simple, Salesman"*, Chicago: Nightingale-Conant, 1974

Hewitt-Gleeson, Dr, Michael, *Software for Your Brain*, Melbourne: Wrightbooks, 1989

    NewSell, Melbourne: Wrightbooks, 1990

    The X10 Memeplex: Multiply Your Business By Ten! Melbourne: Prentice Hall, 2000

Howkins, John, *The Creative Economy*, London: Penguin, 2001

Jaynes, Julian, *The Origin of Consciousness in the Breakdown of the Bicameral Mind*, Boston: Houghton Mifflin, 1976

Jennings, Eugene J., *An Anatomy of Leadership*, New York: McGraw-Hill, 1972

Jones, Landon Y., *Great Expectations*, New York: Ballantine, 1981

Kleinke, Chris L., *Self-Perception*, San Francisco: W. M. Freeman & Coy, 1978

Klivington, Kenneth, *The Science of Mind*, Cambridge MASS: MIT Press, 1989

Levitt, Steven D., and Dubner, Stephen J., *Freakonomics*, Camberwell: Allen Lane, 2005

Locke, Christopher et al, *The Cluetrain Manifesto: The End of Business as Usual*, New York: Perseus, 2000

Maltz, Maxwell, *Psycho-Cybernetics*, Englewood Cliffs, New Jersey: Prentice-Hall, 1960

McKenna, Regis, *The Regis Touch*, Menlo Park CA: Addison-Wesley, 1985

Miller, Gary, and Borgen, C., Winston, *Professional Selling Inside and Out*, New York: Van Nostrand Rinehold, 1979
Miller, James D., *Game Theory At Work*, New York: McGraw-Hill, 2003
Morrison, Philip, *Powers of Ten*, San Francisco: Scientific American Library/W. H. Freeman & Coy, 1982
Ornstein, Robert E., *Psychology of Consciousness*, New York: Penguin/Viking, 1975
& Ehrlich, Paul, *New World New Mind*, London: Methuen, 1989
Potter, Stephan, *The Complete Upmanship*, New York: Plume/NAL, 1978
Ray, Paul H., and Anderson, Sherry Ruth, *The Cultural Creatives*, New York: Harmony Books, 2000
Russell, Frederick A.; Beach, Frank H.; and Buskirk, Richard H., *Textbook of Salesmanship*, 10th ed, New York: McGraw-Hill, 1978
Russell, Peter, *The Brain Book*, New York: E. P. Dutton, 1979
Small, Peter, *The Entrepreneurial Web*, London: Pearson, 2000
Stern, Jim and Priore, Anthony, Email Marketing, New York: John Wiley, 2000
Stone, Bob and Jacobs, Ron, *Successful Direct Marketing Methods*, New York: McGraw-Hill, 2003
Summers Jr., Colonel Harry G., *On Strategy*, New York: Dell, 1984
Suzuki, David, *Genethics*, Sydney: Allen & Unwin, 1988
Sweeney, Susan, *101 Ways To Promote Your Website*, Gulf Breeze: Maximum Press, 2003
Templeton, Tim, *The Referral of a Lifetime*, San Francisco: Berrett-Koehler, 2004
Twain, Mark, *What Is Man?* Thinkers Library No. 60, London: Watts and Co., 1936
Von Baeyer, Hans Christian, *Information: The New Language of Science*, London: Wiedenfeld & Nicolson, 2003
Watson, James D., *DNA: The Secret of Life*, London: William Heinemann, 2003
Welch, Jack, *JACK*, New York: Warner, 2001
Wolfram, Stephen, *A New Kind of Science*, Champaign: Wolfram Media, 2002
Woodcock, Alexallcer, and Davis, Monte, *Catastrophe Theory*, New York: Avon, l980
Young, J. Z. *Programs of the Brain*, London: Oxford University, 1978
Zabin, H., and Mampton, N., *College Salesmanship*, New York: McGraw-Hill, 1970
Zuboff, Shoshana, and Maxmin, James, *The Support Economy*, New York: Penguin, 2002

Index